Wrapped in the Wind's Shawl

Refugees of Southeast Asia and the Western World

Wrapped in the Wind's Shawl

Refugees of Southeast Asia and the Western World

by Scott C. S. Stone
and
John E. McGowan

PRESIDIO PRESS

Copyright © 1980 by Presidio Press

Published by Presidio Press
P.O. Box 3515
San Rafael, CA 94902

Library of Congress Cataloging in Publication Data

Stone, Scott C. S.; 1932–
　Wrapped in the wind's shawl.

　Bibliography:　p.
　1.　Refugees—Indochina.　2.　Refugees—United States.
I.　McGowan, John E., joint author.　II.　Title.
HV640.5.I5S76　　　362.8 ′7 ′0959　　　80-20966
ISBN 0-89141-107-0

Lines from ''Fleeing'' are from *O The Chimneys* by Nelly Sachs,
translated by Ruth and Mathew Mead, Copyright © 1967 by Farrar,
Straus & Giroux, Inc. Reprinted by permission of Farrar, Straus
& Giroux, Inc.

Text and cover design by Mark Jacobson
Typesetting by Publications Services of Marin

Printed in the United States of America

To

Leo Cherne

*who has dedicated more than forty years
of his life to the cause of refugees*

Contents

PART II

Preface

When we undertook to do this book, we knew immediately that there were limitations. The story was too broad to cover in its entirety; the best we could hope for was to show the plight of refugees at a given moment. What we have done is to provide a snapshot of the times, with concentration on Indochina as it was in early 1980. We also knew that our story could be overtaken by events, that the situation would change from month to month and often day to day. We have tried to make this book a blend of history and current reporting, with a look at some of the causes and effects of the refugee movement.

The story of the Indochina refugees had its beginning in events which took place at least 2,000 years ago; we touched on them lightly because of the immediacy of today's happenings. The story has no ending, just as there is not likely to be any quick end to the refugee problem, in Indochina or in the rest of the world. Our aim was to pull together some of the facets of the refugee situation and present them so that readers could have a broad general outline of the reasons why things happened the way they did with regard to thousands of displaced and desperate people.

This book is divided roughly into two parts—the first part, chapters one through seven, is devoted to the situation in Indochina. Chapters eight and nine comprise the second part. These two chapters on worldwide efforts look at the refugee work of the League of Nations, the United Nations agencies and other international organizations, from the Russian Revolution of 1917 through subsequent spasms of inhumanity, intolerance, and insensitivity on the part of governments, dictators, and appeasers. It is less a catalogue of success—and failures—in the business of shifting human cargo, and more a reminder that the root causes of the refugee problem are not present-day phenomena.

Even as the world looks at the refugee situation in Indochina and elsewhere, new refugees are being created. There are three to four times as many persons in a refugee status in Africa than there are in Asia. In April of 1980, with a breathtaking suddenness, or so it seemed, the Russians were in Afghanistan and some two thousand refugees a day were fleeing across the border into Pakistan. The point we want to make is that refugees are a worldwide problem, and one which will not disappear until there is some semblance of world order. Until that day the problem is one which must be considered in terms not only of political actions but also in terms of the human rights every refugee deserves.

Throughout the book we refer to Cambodia instead of Kampuchea. We do so because we feel most people could and would quickly identify that Asian country under the name by which, until recent times, it has been known for decades. We also refer to the states of Laos, Thailand, Burma, Cambodia, and Vietnam as Indochina, and when we use the broader term Southeast Asia, our comments are meant to include Singapore, Malaysia, and the islands of Indonesia.

Some of the book is written in general terms because to be specific about certain facets of Indochina is to court disaster. Almost any statement made can be true somewhere in Indochina and false elsewhere in that area. For despite what Westerners consider a great similarity among the neighboring nations and peoples, there is also a great disparity of customs, thoughts, and ideals. The people of Indochina, indeed of Southeast Asia as a whole, are no more alike than the peoples of Western nations—as dissimilar as a Norwegian from a Spaniard, a Frenchman from a Dutchman. Fortunately, old ideas about Asia are changing rapidly in the West. In the world of *realpolitik* they often change abruptly and sometimes violently. At this writing there is a decided tilt by the United States toward the People's Republic of China, a move bordering on treasonable a few years ago. The first probing suggestions of a China-Japan-U.S. alliance are beginning to be heard. Thailand's ties to the United States appear to be strengthening at this point, while the U.S. attitude toward its former enemy, Vietnam, remains one of coolness.

In some instances in this book, figures seem to vary. This is because in many cases firm data are impossible to obtain. No one knows for sure how many Cambodians died under the excesses of the Pol Pot regime, under the invading Vietnamese, or simply through a lack of sufficient food. Figures vary from two million to four million, depending on the source of information. We have tried to be selective and to keep the figures within hailing distance of each other in a situation best described as fluid. The same holds true for the boat people of Vietnam; either 40 percent or 70 percent died at sea, again depending on where the data came from. Whatever the figure, it represents an appalling loss of human life.

We assume responsibility for any errors of fact. We also want to acknowledge some valuable help. Our thanks go to Paul Wedel and Sylvana Foa of United Press International; to Senators Carl Levin of Michigan and S. I. Hayakawa of California for allowing us to join their entourage briefly on the Thai-Cambodian border, a move that helped us around checkpoints and border guards on a couple of occasions. We want to acknowledge both the background and pleasure we derived from the works of Stanley Karnow and Dennis Bloodworth, among others. Our appreciation also to David J. Roads, Principal Information Officer of the Hongkong Government Information Services, and to James K. Reid and Cheng Puck Fong for their assistance and expertise in the Hongkong camps. Our thanks also go to Margaret Carpenter, Congressional and Public Liaison Officer of the Office of the United States Coordinator for Refugee Affairs, for supplying us with information on U.S. refugee programs; and to the staff of the Public Information Section of the Office of the United Nations High Commissioner for Refugees in Geneva.

This book does not provide the answers to the refugee problem—the response will have to be from the international community—but we hope it accurately and adequately outlines the situation as it was at the time the book was written. We hope too that this work will raise the kinds of questions which will prompt answers from those in positions to give the refugees the kind of aid they must have if they are to rebuild their lives.

Finally, we should state that no refugee program in the United States could succeed as well as it has without the expertise, understanding, compassion, and dedication of the staffs of the private voluntary organizations. The fact that an account of their efforts is only touched on in this work is not in any way to be considered an indication of a lack of recognition.

Honolulu, 1980

Fleeing,
What a great reception
on the way—wrapped
in the wind's shawl
feet in the prayer of sand
which can never say amen . . .

Nelly Sachs
O The Chimneys

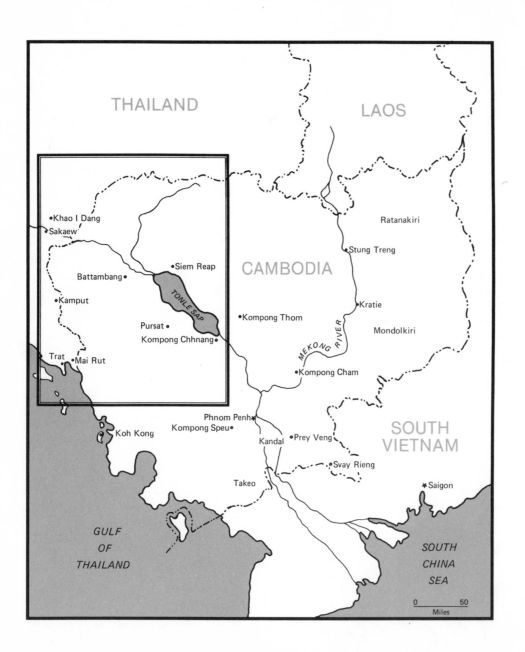

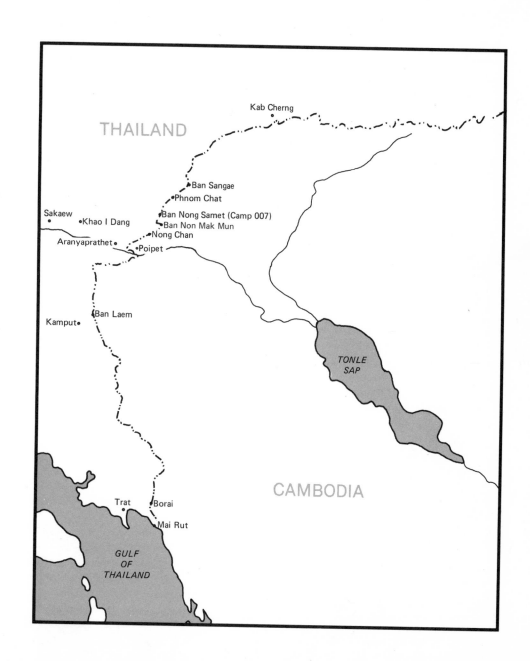

PART I

I

A Tradition of Hatreds

Indochina. The images leap to mind—

A quiet shrine in a strange grotto on a tributary of the great Mekong River, and at the shrine a young girl bends in supplication. From the distance comes the soft sound of a bell, and the sound is caught and held in the grotto, the notes shimmering in the still air.

A stealthy approach by night on an island in the middle of a river, with men in dark clothing lying flat on the deck of a sailing junk. The stars are reflected in the water, the hull creaks as wooden parts rub together. Suddenly there is gunfire from the island, and the battle is joined in an old style naval engagement; broadsides at close range.

A Buddhist monk carrying his begging bowl shuffles down the dusty street of a poor village. When he is offered tea, he carefully covers the cup with a plastic strainer so as not inadvertently to drink any small insects. All life is sacred.

A young boy on a cot at a field hospital of an army unit on the rim of a jungle; he has been bitten by either a cobra or krait, but does not know which. If he is given the wrong antidote, it will kill him. A young doctor takes a guess and administers the antitoxin, then watches helplessly as the boy convulses and dies.

And more—

A small house on stilts on the bank of a river, and in the house is a young Japanese wife, married to a Thai sawmill owner. She sits and nurses a child while watching her husband's workers lead the elephants down to the river to wash in the same water she will have to bathe in later. For this fastidious Japanese girl, it is only one small manifestation of the private hell she suffers for loving a man of another country, and she has spoken quietly to friends of suicide.

A crowd assembles near a loudspeaker on a Bangkok street. It is almost noon. A curious American wanders to the edge of the crowd and asks a question, then smiles at the answer and waits with the crowd. In a few moments he hears the first cheery notes as the King of Thailand launches another solo as a jazz saxophonist.

Indochina. From the air the vast mosaic unfolds in a varied pattern of islands, valleys, mountains, and vibrant cities. From the sweep of the Irrawaddy, across the spine of mountains, and down the exotic shorelines, the land and rivers and villages throw back an image of color and diversity. From the sea, approached on a sailing junk whose design has not changed in a thousand years, the land springs suddenly to life, and the busy shore teems with fishermen and villagers. Beyond the shore the village gives way to the paddies, and beyond the paddies is the jungle, and from the jungle comes an aura of mystery and the scent of murder.

Indochina is complex and exciting. It is mysterious and subtle, brazen and dangerous. Knives flash in the humid nights, but in the long afternoons there is a strange peace in the mountain sanctuaries. Dawn fractures each morning on the spire of the Wat Arun, while in the jungle the banyan roots slowly envelop the remains of monasteries which dwarf anything Europe has produced. In the hill country, in the early mornings, tigers cough, and the sound produces a certain unease even for heavily armed men. Near the soldiers anthropologists nervously carry on their work, trying to piece together the sometimes vivid, sometimes muted, picture of the migrations of peoples and cultures into this strange, shifting, ever-evolving region. Even as they work there is a sense of desperation: who can know the heart and mind of Indochina?

Much of what takes place in Indochina can be explained by the past, by migrations and rivalries, by ethnic, social, political, economic factors. But much is harder to explain. The balance of power shifts in a small village because someone has an automatic weapon. The diverting of a stream brings prosperity to a village but destroys another, but the second village accepts it passively as the way things are. A tame elephant, pulling logs from a teak forest, goes berserk for no discernible reason and tramples a nearby worker. The elephant's owner is beaten to death by enraged coworkers. A police commissioner tells the press that a shoot-out in one of his villages happened because "the men of that village have too much macho." A wealthy owner of a jewelry store in Bangkok inexplicably walks out of his store one sultry morning, dons the saffron robes of a *bonze,* and walks north, never to return.

From April through October the monsoon rains sweep over Indochina; hard, dark rains that chill the body and depress the mind. Thoughts turn to the spirits which dwell in all things. Lakes swell, and villagers dismantle their stilt houses and move them farther from the encroaching water, only to move them back again when the dry season begins at the end of the year. Fish walk across damp land on their fins, looking for food in bigger puddles. New rivers are created and a lake is enlarged to cover hundreds of square miles but to a depth of only five feet. Malaria is rampant, and despite modern drugs, leprosy afflicts thousands of people in villages and hamlets. Altruistic medical men and volunteers from church groups risk death and disease in the dank forests, while corrupt officialdom holds press conferences and takes percentages of aid dollars.

The mood of Indochina is as variable as its different scents. Beneath the gilt surfaces can lie extremes of passion and devotion, and the mellow, soft lighting of late afternoon is deceptive, for guerrillas wait in the jungles, and hate can erupt as quickly as love can die. In the curve of a dancer's arms there is a parallel to the sweep of a blade, and the light of the pale moon, which falls softly over lovers on a canalboat, falls without pity on the body floating in the same canal, the knife with its oddly shaped blade still protruding from the center of the back. With the disappearance of the moon, the sun brings heat and light, glistening from the gilded temples and falling in a gentle blessing over the long stretches of paddies; and in the paddies the children flash white teeth and large, warm brown eyes. The children are as curious as mynah birds and will pick pockets just to see what they contain.

Indochina has its history and its legends, which tend to blur. Archaeologists and anthropologists trace man's presence back half a million years to *Pithecanthropus erectus,* Java man. Not until much later were there masses of humans grouped in the highlands and deltas, and they probably got there before the sea level was raised by melting glaciers of the last ice age separating Indonesia and the Philippines from the continent. The people found a land of contrasts and similarities, a land as confusing as the people themselves. What was to develop, in time, from the varied topography, was a rivalry not only between the region's states, but among the dwellers of the highlands and the wet rice farmers of the lowlands; a case of animosity growing not only horizontally, but vertically.

With the true beginnings lost in antiquity, historians look to a time some forty-five hundred years ago as the beginning of the occupation of the Indochina peninsula. It was the time when a Malay-type people moved into the area and left descendants who mixed with other ethnic strains to form the basic population of Indochina. A legend has it that from the nose of a chieftain's dead buffalo sprang a vine with three pumpkins. When the chieftain burned open one of the pumpkins, he was startled to see men leap out. He quickly cut new openings with a knife to let the rest come forth. The men who came through the burned holes were charred and became the darker, Malay-type peoples. The men who slipped through the knife slashes were the lighter-colored Mongoloids, the Lao. The men went on to domesticate the water buffalo, to develop the methods of rice cultivation, to raise pigs and chickens, to become farmers as well as hunters. In these self-contained communities were planted the seeds of limited loyalties: the hamlet was familiar and friendly and all beyond was menacing. Such suspicions were justified, for the story of Indochina fits the historic pattern of conquest and settlement followed by conquest. All the old jungle fears, the sense of danger, the dark forebodings—all became real.

As on other continents, it was conquest from the north. Out of Central Asia came a tough and tenacious group known simply as the Thai—

the free. They moved in good order to an area of southern China and founded small states along the Yangtze River from Szechwan to the ocean. They were also given to reconnaissance-in-force as far as Vietnam. Pressured by the Chinese, they fought back but in doing so were infused with a certain amount of Chinese culture and outlooks. These sinicized Thai warriors have been given a rare accolade by some historians who believe that if they had possessed a broader economic base they would have overrun China. Instead, they continued to melt into Southeast Asia and along the way were devastated by the Mongols of Kublai Khan, as reported by Marco Polo. In their wake would come fresh waves of migrants, and as in other parts of Indochina, the new migrants would come as warriors who imposed new ideas.

In the first century the important state of Funan occupied much of the peninsula leaving ideas and concepts but few artifacts when it disappeared five hundred years later. At its height the kings of Funan were overlords from the Mekong Delta on the east to the Malay Peninsula on the west. To the north lay the state of Champa, founded two hundred years before Funan by Mongoloid types who came from the north to drive the lowland Malays up into the hills, or to absorb them. It was a short-lived victory, for in 111 B.C. the wiry Han Chinese annexed Champa. As a state Champa disappeared under a thousand years of Chinese domination to reemerge as Vietnam. Now, however, it was greatly sinicized. As Champa was absorbed, the kingdom of Chen-la became dominant. It was a Khmer power, reaching from the southern border of China to modern Cambodia in the south. In the ninth century a Chen-la ruler moved the capital from what may have been the site where Vientiane, Laos, is now located, to a place which would become a household word among archaeologists: Angkor. There a line of kings would, for the next four hundred years, continue to direct the construction of one of the most awe inspiring man-made works in history, a vast complex of tombs, temples, and memorials. When Chen-la itself began to decay, the entire fantastic complex began to be swallowed up by the jungle. A corner of the colossi was uncovered in 1863 by a French naturalist, and much of it has since been rebuilt.

Chen-la fell to the rampaging Thais in the thirteenth century, who were themselves feeling the wrath of the Mongols. As the Thais moved south they ventured into Burma and became known as Shans; they became known as Lao when they conquered and ruled what is now Laos, and were known as

Siamese when they destroyed Angkor and forced the Khmers to move even further to the south. In the mountains of North Vietnam, they retained tribal identities.

The migrations and the wars, the conquests and the exchanges of concepts, the mistrust and skirmishes between highlander and lowlander—all brought a kind of surface similarity to the face of Indochina. Beneath it the ethnic differences continued to keep old animosities alive and volatile. And to these ethnic differences would be added another element: religion.

From India's Coromandel Coast the winter winds swept across the Bay of Bengal to Burma and the Malay Peninsula, on through the Straits of Malacca to Indonesia, or around Singapore and northerly to Indochina. The winds brought Indian traders who were as clever as they were ambitious. Without usurping land, without antagonizing petty kings, and most importantly, without being condescending to primitive tribesmen, the Indians knew a heady success at the timeless and universal law of supply and demand. They also taught the native peoples how to build ports and construct irrigation canals. The Indochinese states began to take on precepts of Indian art and government. And while conquest followed conquest, ruler succeeded ruler, and civilizations fell to be replaced by newer ones, the pervasive concepts of Indian religions took hold.

There was an affinity between the Indochinese belief in a great variety of spirits and the wave of Hinduism which came with the traders. Something stirred in the souls of the villager and fisherman at the idea of Brahma-Vishnu-Siva, the Creator, Preserver, and Destroyer; animistic beliefs were incorporated in the cults, and the many arms of the god seemed to embrace the kingdoms and bestow god-king status on the rulers of the states. Indian epics inspired dancers, artists, and puppeteers. The symbolism and pageantry of those early religious influences are seen all over Indochina today.

In the early centuries A.D. Buddhism also came out of India and washed over Southeast Asia, in particular over what is modern Burma, Laos, Thailand, and Cambodia. It brought with it a social significance, a rejection of the Hindu pantheon and of the priestly power of the Brahmans, and it gave Indochina the Buddhist sage who was recluse, guru, and occasionally social arbiter. Since Buddhism offered peasants a release from repetitive lives of drudgery by promising an end to the endless cycle, it was immensely popular. And because it, too, adapted to the twilight world of spirits, its variant forms began to blur until the concept of *karma* became dominant and the Theravada faith was rooted firmly in Burma, Laos, and Cambodia. Vietnam, the state most influenced by China because of its millennium of Chinese domination, still retained its Mahayana Buddhism but with Chinese overtones and subtleties. In religion, as in other things, Vietnam veered away from its neighbors.

While the Indochinese peninsula early on received its Eastern religions, the Europeans were not to be denied. In 1498 the Portuguese ships of Vasco da Gama rounded the Cape of Good Hope and opened new trade routes in Southeast Asia, and in 1511 Portuguese captured Malacca, the Malayan seaport which was the springboard for other conquests. A decade later Ferdinand Magellan discovered and claimed the Philippines for Spain. The Portuguese had come looking for "Christians and spices" and the Spanish for trade and prestige. They would be followed by the British, the French, the Dutch. In addition to all other influences, the Westerners brought yet another religion, Christianity. And to the south of the Indochina peninsula, sun swept islands beneath the wind, the roots of Islam were planted by Moslem traders who moved a trading center from the Indian port of Cambay to Malacca, in Malay Indonesia.

In much of Indochina, then as now, the varying religions were like coats of lacquer, one on another and often mixing. To draw a straight and consistent line from the origins of each religion to the practice of it in the villages would be impossible, for in each murky twist and turn are seen the dim outlines of other ancient beliefs, until at last they blend like smoke.

Like religion, another great force flowed through the lives and psyches of the Indochinese, bringing sustenance and hope. It began beyond the far-off Himalayas, sixteen thousand feet high on the Tibetan plateau where snow fed sources produced what the Tibetans called Dza-Chu, the Water of the Rocks. As it tumbled south through China, the river was called Lan-Tsan Kiang, the Turbulent River. It crossed into Indochina at a collision of Burma, Laos, Thailand, and China and before emptying into the South China Sea had flowed twenty-six hundred miles. The Vietnamese called it Cuu Long Giang, the River of the Nine Dragons, for its nine major tributaries. The Khmer called it Tonle Thom, the Big Water. The Lao and Thai, who share a common tongue, spoke of the "mother river khong" not being able to define precisely what khong means. Westerners, ever impatient, made a contraction and called it the Mekong.

In monsoon floods the Mekong brought rich alluvial soil and abundant crops of rice. The face of Indochina was squared into neat paddies, and the ubiquitous water buffalo drew harrows, preparing the soil for planting. Fishermen went into the café au lait water to place their fishnets. People used the waterways for transportation and to go marketing. In the rainy season the great Mekong in flood could produce as much as five thousand miles of new and uncharted waterways, small canals which could be skimmed in light craft. In places the river flowed backwards as the seasons alternated, and for thousands of years the people who lived within the touch of the Mekong adapted the rhythm of their lives to the monsoons and the mighty river.

As constant as the river flowed the rivalries.

One style of writing the word Indochina is Indo-China, and the hyphen falls on Vietnam. Laos, Cambodia, Thailand, and Burma retain more of the Indian and Malay cultures and religions, but beyond the hyphen to the east Vietnam is more under the Chinese influence in its traditions, its religions, and its governmental forms. In the Indo part of Indochina there is a certain languor missing from Vietnam, and it is in Vietnam that the Malay-type homes on stilts disappear (except on waterways where tides or flooding make them necessary). It would be easy to contend that Vietnam was at war with its sister states because of this veneer of Chinese suzerainty, that cultural shadings alone provided the impetus for dispute. The flaw in this argument is that the other states have just as long a litany of warfare, border disputes, shifting loyalties, and violence upon each other.

Cambodian hostility to Vietnam dates back to the earlier settlements and reached furious proportions in the fifteenth century following the Vietnamese conquest and occupation of Champa. In the same century, Cambodian-Thai relations were on a wartime footing; the newly established Thai state of Ayuthia destroyed Angkor. In a land of long memories, Cambodia looks both east and west and sees reminders of its devastation.

In what today is Laos there was a persistent resistance to becoming the vassals of the Thais, although the people were ethnically tied. And the area around Vientiane was a pocket of that resistance. Another was Luang Prabang which, however, discovered it preferred the Thais to the periodic invasions by the Burmese and the Vietnamese. Even within Laos itself, the fervent animists, the Black Thai, resisted any controls from the Lao of the lower Mekong area. So did the hill tribes; the Kha, Meo, Man, and Moi.

In Thailand (Siam) there was a tradition of command. The descendants of the hardy Thais from Central Asia carried the genes of conquerors and ruled great parts of Burma almost as often as the Burmese did. Additionally, the Thais encroached on the Lao as vigorously as the Lao resisted. Not always successful, the Thais suffered a devastating blow from Burmese invaders in the mid-eighteenth century, and the memory persists in the collective mind of Thailand.

Throughout this turbulent history the peoples of Indochina looked north with trepidation toward the reality of China, while China looked south on who it considered the *nan-man,* the southern barbarians. In a real sense the Indochinese themselves were living proof of the vigor of migrations from the north, and the possibility of stirring the sleeping giant colored much of the thought and some of the political moves of Southeast Asia. It was a situation which would persist right into modern times.

But if they looked north, the Indochinese also looked west. And with good reasons.

The Portuguese and Spanish traders came, bringing trade, prejudices, Christianity, and a competitive zeal: they meant to stop both the Arab trade and the spread of Islam. In Indonesia they were closely followed by the Dutch who took Malacca from the Portuguese in the early seventeenth century and carved out an unenviable reputation for exploitation. By 1824 the British were in control of Penang, Malacca, and a tiny dot off the Malay Peninsula called Singapore. When a monarch of Burma threatened to take over portions of British India, the British took portions of Burma instead as well as a good bit of the Malay Peninsula. After more than three hundred years of Spanish rule, the Americans reluctantly accepted the Philippines in 1898, with President McKinley commenting ruefully, "The truth is, I didn't want the Philippines . . . there was nothing left for us to do but take them all, and to educate the Filipinos . . ." The French pushed into Indochina in 1871 motivated by a search for la gloire and the restoration of national pride following her defeat by Prussia. In time she could write French Indochina across a land that once had known the temples of Champa.

The push by the West into Indochina was neither concerted effort nor master-planned. The French came with hauteur and an irresistible Gallic culture; the Americans came grumbling about it all but keen for trade all the same; the Dutch came with an eye for profit; the English with several muddled philosophies and tremendous energies; and the Spanish and Portuguese with a certain rapacious zeal. What they shared, with two notable exceptions, was an inability or unwillingness to build a strong management class of successors, perhaps in the mistaken belief that they were in permanent and enduring strongholds. The notable exceptions were the United States, which embarked on a policy of someday vacating the Philippines, and England, which created a legislative council in Burma and put Burmese in important civil service posts.

The effect of all this was to inspire nationalism without creating nations. The peoples of Indochina were emerging into the modern world in a displacement of many of their values and some of their history—a case of being pulled not only into another culture but almost into another age. If there were stirrings of nationalism, they were surpressed, often ruthlessly. Colonialism became more than a word, and the boundaries fixed by Western powers were artificial ones by Indochinese historical standards. For a time the West was supreme and Western ideals seemed irreversible. The sun never set on the Union Jack or on many another Western flag.

Then it was an Asian flag that suddenly triumphed. In 1905 the Japanese battle ensign flew above the flagship of Admiral Togo, whose fleet took on the Russian Baltic Fleet in the Tsushima Straits and devastated the tsar's thirty-eight ships. Combined with the defeat of the Russian army in the Russo-Japanese War, it badly damaged the myth of Western superiority. For more than three decades Southeast Asia remained in the status quo, but nationalistic feelings were being encouraged by zealots who dreamed of independence. There was occasional rioting, but no significant changes until the Japanese, once again, precipitated change. Crying "Asia for the Asians," the Japanese fell with brutal efficiency on Southeast Asia.

Thailand survived uncolonized by declaring war on the Allies and allowing Japan to use the country for an assault on Malaya. The Japanese simply took over the rest of Southeast Asia until the fortunes of war once again forced them out. With their departure came the full-throated cry for independence. The legacy left by the Japanese was a reputation for brutality, a sense of organization, and a spirit of collectivism.

World War II spelled the end of European authority in Indochina. The Labor government of Britain knew it and agreed to freedom for Burma. It came on 4 January 1948. Two years earlier the United States, in an emotional ceremony, lowered the Stars and Stripes from over the Philippines and saluted the flag of a new and independent Republic of the Philippines. For other nations, letting go was more difficult. There was bloody rioting in Java where Indonesians fought the Dutch; then after four wracking years, the Netherlands agreed to an independent Indonesia in 1949.

Asians were talking nationalism.

As it had so many times in the past, Vietnam found itself in a different position from its neighbors. There was one brief, shining moment—and it came in March of 1946—when the French Commissioner in Hanoi and the highly respected Ho Chi Minh agreed to a Democratic Republic of Vietnam; one which would retain its French ties and enjoy its independence within the French community. The Vietnamese self-destruct syndrome came into full play; extremists in both camps sabotaged the agreement, and the opening shots were fired in 1946, in a conflict which was not to let up until eight years later.

In that eight-year cycle of warfare, East and West began to take the measure of each other. Along the dank trails with their jungle canopies and through the passes of the highlands, the Vietminh of Ho Chi Minh and the French professional soldiers clashed in brief, savage firefights or fought set piece battles. The last such battle came at Dien Bien Phu in 1954, when Vietminh guerrillas finally brought the Tricolor to the ground. French political moves suffered the same fate. Having enticed Bao Dai to set up a government to the south, the French found that the playboy emperor was no match for the flinty, revered Ho Chi Minh. Ho emerged as the leader of the Communist movement, which now controlled the nationalist movement entirely. North Vietnam was effectively Communist and eyeing its neighbors to the south.

In Saigon, the Vietnamese looked north, again with concern. The Geneva Conference of 1954 had cut Vietnam into two portions with an arbitrary slash along the 17th Parallel, and many educated and technically trained Vietnamese were in the north. South Vietnam's President, Ngo Dinh Diem, knew his government lacked enough competent personnel; a situation complicated by the fact that every wind from the north seemed to bring agitators and infiltrators. It was just a matter of time until broader clashes came about, and to help the South Vietnamese, America sent advisors. Initially they were limited to a training role which was later modified to a "fire when fired upon" rule. This unrealistic dictum was largely ignored by the Americans, and they took active part in skirmishes against the Communist led movement in the South known as the National Liberation Front—the Viet Cong.

America went to Vietnam scarcely guessing the intricacies and patterns of ensuing events. Diem became more and more of a recluse until he was assassinated, to be followed by a succession of leaders and generals who attempted to lead. The situation was chaotic and the war dragged on, with the United States pouring aid money into the war efforts (and into some governmental pockets) and committing thousands of young men. Like the French, the Americans were suddenly bogged down in a Vietnam war that seemed unending. Ironically, it was now the French calling for the Americans to get out of Vietnam. So too were demonstrators in America, and the conflict in far-off Indochina split families in the United States, sending some young men to Canada and Sweden and ending in a legacy of bitterness on the part of Vietnam veterans who had done what they considered the honorable thing to do. With Vietnamization the catch-phrase, America began to withdraw, leaving innumerable tons of equipment in the hands of the South Vietnamese. Inevitably, the country fell to the tough and energetic northerners, and the last American presence many South Vietnamese saw was the helicopters leaving the American embassy. The northerners wasted no time in beginning a reeducation process for the recalcitrant southerners. Some were moved into education camps, some were simply eliminated.

With the establishment of a Communist government over a unified Vietnam, Communist forces spilled over into neighboring countries in a familiar reprise of the past two thousand years. Laos came under control of the Vietnamese with startling speed. The wily, and now highly experienced, Vietnamese army rolled into Cambodia and ran headlong into the savage Khmer Rouge (Cambodian Communists). Despite the same ideological labels, the old hatreds flared, and again there was the ancient tradition confirmed: the states of Indochina were locked in combat. With the Vietnamese still tearing around in the north, a series of leaders arose and disappeared in Phnom Penh. The mercurial Prince Norodom Sihanouk was in favor, out of favor, in Beijing and out again; he was everywhere but in control of Cambodia. Lon Nol came into power and went out again, to settle for a time in a pleasant neighborhood in Hawaii before moving on to the U.S. Mainland. Pol Pot became premier of Cambodia; then for four years he tore the country apart with near genocidal ruthlessness in his attempts to eliminate both the Vietnamese and any resistance to his regime. Meanwhile a Khmer Serei (Free Khmer) movement grew, opposed to Pol Pot and equally opposed to the Vietnam supported government of the new ruler, Heng Samrin, in now devastated Phnom Penh. Occasionally the Khmer Serei fought among themselves.

In Laos, the storied "land of a million elephants," Vietnam tightened its hold on the government and issued shoot-to-kill orders against anyone attempting to leave the country. In the dark tradition of Indochina, the Communists began a systematic drive to transform Laos into a Vietnamese colony. (One result has been that much of the rice grown to feed needy villagers in Laos is used instead to supply the rampaging Vietnamese army and its estimated fifty thousand garrison troops in Laos.)

Amid the violent winds that ranged across Indochina's history was the faint whiff of burning joss sticks. Another ethnic group had centuries ago moved down into Indochina and spread like the widening waters of the Mekong. The ethnic Chinese traversed borders and waterways and established themselves throughout the peninsula; they were canny, persistent, and successful. They faced a variety of persecutions and prohibitions, but that merely stimulated their drive for land, money, and power. They got into a great deal of trouble in Indonesia and the Philippines, and in Indochina they clutched their culture and thought of the Middle Kingdom. They called themselves *hua chiao*—the sojourning Chinese—and their hard work set them apart from many of the more indolent Southeast Asians. They built up interests in agriculture and small businesses, finding the needs and filling them. They expanded into mining and transportation and on into banking and finance. They were loved and hated, damned, and sought out as a source of funds. They ranged from backward villages to the back seats of Mercedes and Daimlers, and all the while they wrapped their heritage around them like a protective cloak. They studied the turbulent regimes around them and steadfastly held onto their independence, forming Chinese islands in the stream of Indochinese humanity. But when the Communists' blow fell, they too, like the indigenous peoples of Laos, Vietnam, and Cambodia, were caught between the hammer and the anvil. When their loyalties came into question, it became obvious that the overseas Chinese, the sojourning Chinese, were loyal primarily to themselves.

By the end of 1975 the great question in Indochina was no longer one of loyalties but one of survival. Cambodia, now Kampuchea, was savaged by bloody fighting. The reports of atrocities in Cambodia evoked history's basest moments. Stories out of Vietnam were also tales of oppression, and around the world the old Asia hands nodded their heads—the Indochinese penchant for doing damage to each other was manifesting itself again. To much of the bewildered world, it was impossible to understand such brutality. How could a region washed by Hinduism, Buddhism, Christianity, Islam, and the teaching of Confucius writhe in such blood and terror? How can a people, who will save small insects from being consumed in a cup of tea, let other people die in such agony and in such numbers?

The answers are as murky as the sudden night which drops like a curtain over Indochina. Perhaps among the spirits there are capricious and uncaring ones. The monsoons are depressing. The rice crop failed. Someone had a gun in an up-country village; the phrase to run amok came from Southeast Asia. The dreary repetition of village life in some areas, the heat, the disease, the lack of hope—all could be contributing factors. It may be that people who are extremely devout are, indeed, extremists and thus capable of enormous cruelty. Perhaps it is the very religiosity of such lives that gives the extremism its great fury. At the very least, there is a tradition of hatreds in Indochina that today has resulted in yet another period of war and human misery, and has launched the mind-boggling exodus of people from Vietnam, Laos, and Cambodia.

Since the Communist takeover in much of Indochina, more than one and a half million people have left their homes and begun the terrible search for land and life. Some of them fled in a search for freedom, some were pushed out because they were dissidents, some—the ethnic Chinese—were forcibly evacuated, and some left for fear of reprisals.

What the world looked at was the terrible television footage of infants with swollen bellies and thin limbs, children who would be dead in a matter of days. The front pages of newspapers carried, for a time, photos of the young mothers, soon to die, and the old people, covered with dirty cloths, resigned to death. A flat gaze, inheritor of centuries of cruelties, stared right back at the viewer. It was a gaze that asked for help but did not really expect it. For if it is difficult to know the heart and mind of Indochina, is it any easier to know the soul of the rest of humanity?

II

The Thai-Cambodian Border

In the early morning darkness we left Bangkok and headed east toward the border between Thailand and Cambodia. A strange, dense fog hung over the city, and well out into the countryside and through it, at dawn, a blood red sun called attention to itself but gave off no heat and little light. In the country the fog seemed whiter and much thicker. Occasionally we would come across huge crows sitting on the power lines alongside the road, as black in the fog as pencilmarks on a white sheet of paper. Once we scared them up from the carcass of a dog lying in the road, its neck broken by a passing vehicle. The morning was full of signs and portents; the sun was ominous instead of comforting, and the trees alongside the road threw back strange shapes and shadows. Now and then a temple would rise out of a field, dimly visible but adding a grace note to a morning which seemed to be holding its breath.

We were accompanied by Sylvana Foa, Indochina Manager for United Press International, and Barry Flynn, a free-lancer working out of Bangkok. Our driver and interpreter was Suiaphol, a Bangkok native who regarded everything outside the city limits as frontier country, but whose curiosity about the camps impelled him to volunteer to hurl us eighty miles eastward in his Toyota, with his collection of Elton John tapes near to hand. The jumping-off place for the camps was the important, if small, border town of Aranyaprathet, with its euphonious name and its convenient location just inside Thailand along the border with Cambodia. We reached it without incident and in a clearing fog, and all at once it was cloudless and hot. A few miles further we reached the refugee camp of Khao I Dang.

"You won't see any starving babies or dying people here," Sylvana Foa had said earlier, and she was right. But what we saw were 107,000 people who had made the journey into the heart of darkness and were coming out the other side—and most of them scarred from the experience, and all of them homeless. Having faced the prospect of dying from hunger, the survivors now had other problems, some more subtle. And the atmosphere of the camp was one of watchful waiting.

The first complex of buildings housed the United Nations relief organizations, medical people, teachers, and administrators. The flags of Thailand and the United Nations hung limply in the windless morning thirty feet above the headquarters complex. Behind the parking area was a gate manned by Thai soldiers, and just inside the gate were more soldiers and a jeep with a mounted machine gun. As we took our first look around the camp, more refugees came in from another camp, moved for one reason or another. The first procedure involving these new refugees was for the Thai soldiers to search their possessions and throw into a pile all the hatchets, digging tools, and other sharp instruments. The Thai soldiers here have long memories of "incidents" in the camp in which people have died. At first it was hard to believe that people who had fled from certain death would take part in violence of any kind in a refugee camp, but while we were there we heard that the night before some soldiers had found a group of refugee men gambling and had routinely tried to break up the game. The soldiers were jumped by the gamblers and beaten so severely that one of them was hospitalized. A contingent of Thai soldiers, armed, went back to "punish" the gamblers, but no one would tell us what happened after that. We let it go and walked out into the camp itself.

Khao I Dang is built on a dry, hot, waterless stretch of border area; everything in it is covered with a fine, powdery dust. To supply this camp and the other border camps with water costs thirteen thousand dollars per day. The water is trucked up in convoys, put into holding containers, and pumped through pipes to the various sections of camp. Water is scarce and not wasted. The camp itself—the so-called houses, beds, latrine shields, even some of the utensils—is made from bamboo. The houses are simply thatched huts big enough to sleep in. The crowding is appalling, even by rural Asian standards, and new areas are constantly being cleared for incoming refugees. The camp is virtually treeless, and the only escape from the pitiless sun is inside the huts. The people now look adequately fed, compared to a few weeks earlier when the bloated bellies and vacant eyes spoke of advanced malnutrition, the prelude to death. Now they eat rice and a kind of stew which is highly nutritious, and sometimes canned fish. Medical teams supplied by the United Nations High Commissioner for Refugees (UNHCR) are always on duty. In one area there were wooden buildings being readied for use as schoolrooms.

The refugees cannot leave the camp without a reason. The Thai government is uneasy with the fact of 450,000 foreign refugees crowding its borders in some fifteen camps, and it tries to contain them as much as possible. Responsibility for doing so is divided between the Thai army and marines, and everywhere there are Thai troops in green or camouflage uniforms carrying American made M-16s and .45s. Implicit in the presence of the troops is the belief of the Thais that the loosing of refugees across Southeast Asia is a deliberate policy of the Vietnamese government to solve several of its pressing problems by dumping the refugees elsewhere. Relationships between the Thais and the refugees is roughly comparable to that between the guards and the inmates of any large prison.

The most striking thing about the Khao I Dang camp is the children. There are thousands of them, unfailingly good-humored and curious about visitors. In early 1980 the camp began to reverse a trend, and there were more children being born than people dying. Everywhere, the children crowd at any excuse; if a child stops to look at an unusual rock in the dusty lanes between housing areas, a crowd of them will gather. When visitors try to photograph one child, suddenly there are five or six in the viewfinder and more running to be in the picture. They shout hello, hello and okay and bye-bye. They have makeshift toys, including kites made from the plastic sheeting that contains some of their supplies. They carve crude vehicles out of plastic containers, fit them out with wheels of small tin cans, and pull these rolling toys around the camp on strings. We saw one soccer game in progress, the ball being a blown up plastic bag with a string tied around the top. The children, excited as they were by the game, were careful not to kick it too hard. And all the time they dash around like children everywhere, laughing and kicking up dust, and looking upward to the adults with enormous brown eyes and a quick smile. Some of them have known nothing but the camp, and some of them are orphans, and they all face an uncertain future. But they have quicksilver laughter, and they dart like sparrows, and it is impossible not to get caught up in their games or share in their sudden smiles.

The young people and adults are a different story. They wear a strange assortment of clothing, some of it obviously designed for winter weather, some of it advertising tourist destinations which are inconceivable to the adults. They walk warily through the camp, and their eyes are watchful. They do not smile as readily as the children, and one senses that such reserve is not usual for these once carefree people. They sit near their huts and stare without expression out into the lanes between the sections of camp. Occasionally they play a kind of game with round balls similar to the Italian game of bocce, but the game we watched seemed to generate only a few smiles and none of the boisterous laughter that once characterized any group of Cambodians at play. This same kind of apathy would be seen in other camps, and U.N. officials believe it is an outgrowth of both terror and boredom; it is in any case a kind of trauma which may be striking enough, and common enough, to earn its way into new psychiatric studies.

We sat on an outcropping of rocks near the northern end of the camp and tried to see it as a refugee would. The barren, baking landscape was depressing, the huts crowded and lacking privacy. There would be enough food and water but nothing to quicken the spirit or bring joy to the heart. In the rainy season it would be a quagmire. Going to the bathroom meant squatting next to your neighbor over a long row of slit trenches shielded from people passing nearby only by a series of woven mats about four feet high. Smoke from cooking fires hung for long moments in the still air, and all the *farangs* (foreigners) we saw were sweating in the merciless heat. Near the water containers, people were bathing by sluicing water over themselves, the men still in shorts, the women in saronglike garments which would be replaced deftly and without exposure by a dry one, in the way of rural Indochinese women accustomed to the same style of bathing in rivers. In one corner of a housing section, a middle-aged barber with one small mirror and one pair of scissors was cutting hair and talking constantly. A car rolled by slowly with U.N. medical personnel, and the dust from the car rose and hung, and had just dissipated when the car came back. Two children were playing with marbles near the side of the dirt road—but they had only one marble each, so the game was simply one trying to hit the other's marble in turn.

If there was boredom, there was at least enough food. In the storage area behind the U.N. complex were tons of rice and other goods. Monthly food rations for each refugee adult and child have been standardized both by amount and type. The diet consists mainly of rice, meat, vegetables, fish sauce, and seasonings. In establishing this diet, the World Health Organization was consulted. The general opinion of visitors to the camp is that after the bitter period of starvation and death, the residents of Khao I Dang now have more than just the minimum required for survival, and that in many cases their diet is more nutritious than that of the average Indochinese. In establishing the ground rules for letting these thousands of people take asylum on the soil of Thailand, the Thai government specified that the refugees' lifestyles would not exceed that of the local Thais; so certain standards were set for food, water, shelter, and medical care. There was an agreement that the UNHCR personnel would monitor the distribution of food, and it was discovered that in some camps the rations were being sold by the refugee committees which were in charge of distribution. We heard no such tales now in Khao I Dang, although such reports were common in all camps during the first phase of the refugee exodus.

Despite the availability of food, there is fear among the medical people that the children may have suffered brain damage because of severe and prolonged malnutrition. And at Khao I Dang we heard the first worried comments about the mental health of the children. A nurse told us that the children had bad dreams, and that on the rare occasions when the older children had pencil and paper, their drawings were harsh and angular and often dealt with guns and explosions. Many of the older ones were silent and withdrawn.

Perhaps they have good reason, for in Khao I Dang we also heard the first tales of the continuing rivalries taking place, even among people who have lost their land, their homes, and in many cases, significant parts of their families. While it did not seem to be prevalent in the Khao I Dang camp, we were told wild stories of raids between camps, of rivalries within the Khmer Serei (Free Khmer) which resulted in shoot-outs. We heard of a Thai bombardment of one of the camps which went on for several hours in efforts to quell a disturbance—at least the Thais were blamed for it. In the sometimes shadowy world of the border camps, facts are more difficult to obtain now than food. We heard stories of the mad prince in another camp, and of Khmers slipping back across the border into Cambodia to join in guerrilla actions against the Vietnamese invaders; an action which may invite retaliation and lead to deeper involvement by the Thai troops. It was not a situation calculated to make anyone optimistic, but as it turned out, Khao I Dang was probably the most controlled and peaceful of the border camps near Aranyaprathet, because when we tried to get into the next camp near the Thai village of Ban Nong Samet, we were turned back by Thai soldiers who told us we were being denied entry for our own safety.

The camp is called Camp 007, because of its many intrigues. Its camp leader is a controversial figure named In Sakhan, a politician-soldier of the Khmer Serei. Only the preceding weekend, In Sakhan had led some of his troops in a pitched battle with other Cambodians, presumably refugees who had been Khmer Rouge guerrillas. There was undoubtedly a series of clashes, and there were reports of casualties. The Thais were furious. They knew there were at least one thousand active Khmer Serei troops in Camp 007, and they could foresee other battles raging along the border. Finally, on a calm Sunday evening, In Sakhan surrendered to the Thai Third Infantry Battalion in Aranyaprathet, ending yet another episode in the murky world of border rivalries. It would not be the last. Days after the clash we were still unable to get into the camp near Ban Nong Samet.

What we did find was some fifty thousand Cambodians in knockdown, temporary quarters of matting and cloth some distance from the permanent camp. They were extremely wary, and we were accompanied by armed Thai troops on a walk through the temporary encampment. The conditions were nearly indescribable. There was no thought given to sanitation, no attempt made to provide privacy, and a seeming unconcern on the part of the occupants for anything except getting back to their permanent camp. The camp commander told us he hoped to get the entire contingent back into the camp before nightfall, which seemed overly optimistic. Meanwhile, out on the dirt road bordering the encampment, Thai troops sat in jeeps and behind machine guns. They seemed edgy and were relieved when we left the camp. It was in this temporary encampment that we saw probably the most piteous child, a little girl recovering very slowly from months of malnutrition and hunger. She was small and thin, and her eyes held a vacant look. We thought she was holding a black belt, but when we got closer we saw that it was a long bone, stripped clean of meat but so covered with flies it was hardly recognizable. She clutched it with both hands and moved away from us as we drew closer. When she moved she did not turn her back but backed away until she was lost in the crowd.

A reporter who had been inside Camp 007 a few days earlier described the scene as quiet but desolate; 250,000 people demoralized by the fighting in which In Sakhan's forces apparently were forced into a defensive battle during the last phase of the attack—by Cambodian forces still unidentified. The reporter said the final attack lasted about five hours and involved mortars, rockets, AK-47 and M-16 automatic weapons, and American made M-79 grenade launchers. On the way out of the camp, the reporter and his party came across an unidentified dead woman, killed by gunfire. They cremated her. Later, on the outskirts of the camp, they saw combat troops who said they belonged to a faction led by another Cambodian camp commander, Van Saren. They were, they said, en route to attack Khmer Rouge forces loyal to Pol Pot. Trying to sort it out, the reporter, a native Thai, still was unable to determine exactly who the invaders were who had attacked (or were attacked by) the In Sakhan forces and now were to be rescued by the Van Saren forces. One of the more startling rumors was that the attackers were actually Khmer Rouge who had gone over to the Vietnamese forces now occupying Cambodia. These currents and crosscurrents, these rivalries and grasps for power in the border camps, provide some justification for the frustrations of the Thai government and military, who regard the refugees as interlopers and want nothing more than for all of them to get off Thai soil and go home.

Even as officials were questioning camp commanders and trying to bring some order out of the confusion, fresh fighting broke out in other areas along the border. Residents of two Cambodian villages near Aranyaprathet, Phnom Malai and Phnom Mark Huen, reported heavy gunfire in the predawn hours. They said that soldiers of the Vietnamese backed puppet ruler of Cambodia, Heng Samrin, took up positions on a mountainside on the Cambodian side of the border and opened fire into a valley with mortars and machine guns. A day later, residents of Aranyaprathet heard the crunch of mortars and 105mm howitzers on the Cambodian side of the border. Refugees fleeing the area said a group of Khmer Serei soldiers had killed five

Heng Samrin troops who were among Cambodians fleeing into a Khmer Serei camp. Such combat discomfits the Thais, who are worried about a larger problem. They fear that so many Khmers will find sanctuary on the Thai side of the border that the Heng Samrin government, under prodding from Hanoi, will be compelled to launch attacks in violation of Thailand's territorial integrity, and that the Thais will have to respond. It explains in part the animosity that the Thais feel toward the entire refugee situation, and that coupled with the centuries-old rivalries in Indochina makes for considerable tension in the camps. During the entire rainy season, from April until late October, the Thais lived with the fear of a Vietnamese attack coming in the dry season, usually November to May. This fear was shared by almost everyone, including some officials in Washington. In late December 1979, State Department officials said there was no evidence the Vietnamese were planning a large-scale offensive, but others in Washington expected an offensive against the Khmer Rouge and/or Khmer Serei forces which, they felt, would violate Thailand's border and precipitate a wider action. Thailand is allied to the United States by the 1954 Manila Treaty which set up the now disbanded Southeast Asia Treaty Organization (SEATO). In 1962, a joint statement by the United States and Thailand made it more specific; the United States will lend full support to Thailand in the event of Communist aggression. On 12 December 1979, President Carter noted that the United States would meet its commitment to Thailand, and other administration sources said the United States would provide military aid if the war spilled over into Thailand.

So the Thais guard the refugee camps as best they can and gaze over the border into Vietnamese-occupied Cambodia, where at least 180,000 battle-tested Vietnamese troops continue their drive against Cambodian guerrillas. The Thais are fully aware that the Vietnamese forces are supplied by the Soviet Union, while the Cambodian forces are backed by the People's Republic of China, and are even more distressed by the realization that the war may be nothing more than a proxy war between the two superpowers. Or nothing less.

There was some relief in mid-January 1980, when the Hanoi government announced to a group of visiting Americans that there would not be an offensive during the dry season. The announcement, by Deputy Foreign Minister Phan Hien, was significant in itself, but it was coupled with statements which indicated the Vietnamese had no intention of leaving

Cambodia. He said the Vietnamese had the duty to organize a new society since the old one had been destroyed. He told the American delegation, headed by Rep. Lester Wolff, a New York Democrat who chairs the House Subcommittee on Asian and Pacific Affairs, that Vietnamese troops would stay in Cambodia "as long as necessary," and then he launched a verbal attack on Thailand. He said the Thais should not permit sanctuaries inside the Thai border, and he insisted that the Thai military screen persons fleeing Cambodia to weed out the true refugees and turn back into Cambodia the guerrillas seeking temporary refuge. Phan Hien also expressed his displeasure with the apparent U.S. tilt toward China. The minister closed his discussion by saying that he considered the Khmer guerrillas a spent force, and that Vietnamese actions were now simply mopping-up operations. This was a viewpoint not shared by Thai military officers, who claimed the 20,000 Khmer guerrillas would continue to harass the 180,000 to 200,000 Vietnamese troops in Cambodia when the rainy season began again. Meanwhile, in the dry season, they were lying relatively low. The dry season allows the Vietnamese army to maneuver more troops and tanks and artillery pieces against the Cambodian infantry, but in the rainy season it becomes primarily an infantry-to-infantry action without the larger weapons. On the political front in the dry season, the Khmer Rouge leaders took another step. They ousted Pol Pot, whose excesses during four years of rule had cost the lives of hundreds of thousands, perhaps millions, of Cambodians. Both for their world image and for internal reasons, Pol Pot was replaced by the reportedly more moderate Khieu Samphan as premier but was retained as supreme commander of the military forces.

Only a month before the upheaval at Camp 007 near Ban Nong Samet, the camp had been described by United Press International as "well-organized and free from strife," unlike, said UPI, the Khmer Serei camp at Ban Non Mak Mun. It was to the latter camp in the late afternoon that Suiaphol, our driver, pointed his now grimy Toyota. Running low on gasoline and covered in the red dust thrown up by the jeepful of Thai escort soldiers, we pulled up in front of the camp and entered a world of tension and a heightened sense of menace.

The first feeling was one of slight disorientation; of not knowing exactly where we were. The second was the realization that dusk was approaching, and the sun had taken on that ominous coloration shimmering dully through the gathering haze. A sudden sense of menace made us uneasy. We went into the headquarters compound and talked briefly with the camp commander. Above his head was a crude drawing of Rosalynn Carter, with Oriental eyes, holding a baby. There was also the fierce green and red demon insignia of the Khmer Serei, glowering at visitors. After a while we left the compound and started walking through the camp.

The air seemed to crackle with tension but through it came a very human odor, the ripe smell from the nearby latrines mixed with the smoky scent of cooking fires. The camp, home to some 140,000, appeared to have little concern for sanitation. Clouds of flies hung about every hut, and discarded food scraps and broken bits of melon were covered with them. But it was the faces and the eyes which lent the scene its menace. As we walked through the camp, there were fewer smiles than we had seen in other places. The children were less boisterous, and if they got in front of our little procession the adults did not laugh about it as they did in other camps. Instead, some adult, always a male, would growl an order, and the children would melt away from our path. We moved through an ocean of faces, most of them blank and unsmiling, but with cold and cautious eyes. There was no overt act, but there was the realization that the camp was volatile and unpredictable, and danger was in the air.

At one point we noted that we must be very close to Cambodia. "You're standing in it," Sylvana Foa said. "We entered Cambodia when we crossed the ditch back there."

In one corner of the camp we came across a strange contingent—a group of some fifty or sixty Vietnamese who had taken up refuge in the camp. We asked if they were well-treated and well-fed, and their spokesman, looking at the expressionless face of the camp commander, said yes, of course; they were well-treated, and the food they received was free, and the camp commander ran a very good camp indeed. We thought about the racial tensions of Indochina and the instability of this particular camp, and we wondered what the spokesman might have said had we been able to get him alone.

We headed back toward the entrance to the camp, walking over rough terrain and around the housing sections, which seemed more haphazard and unplanned than the other camps. Two months earlier there had been considerable fighting in this camp, with the initial attack apparently coming from the Cambodian side of the camp and started by a difference of opinion as to the camp's future. One faction wanted to stay in Cambodia and fight the Vietnamese, and the other opted to return to Thailand and sanctuary. The latter faction wanted to move the camp inside Khao I Dang. Among the inhabitants of the camp, many of the men were armed with automatic weapons, and the Thai troops claim quarrels and infighting are frequent.

As we left the camp's housing area we were suddenly struck by the silence of the camp. Cambodians are normally a gregarious people, given to talk and banter and easy discourse. Part of that electric tension in the air undoubtedly came from the silence, and the silence itself from the trauma most of these people have suffered. That, and the knowledge that they were still fighting the Vietnamese or each other and their war was not yet over. In Ban Non Mak Mun, as in other camps, there remains the basic question for each Cambodian refugee—to try to emigrate, or to return to Cambodia and fight the Vietnamese invaders.

Emigration, for most, would be very difficult because they have no relatives or ties abroad. Few of them have any skills other than simple farming, and that the highly specialized farming of Indochina. Many of them cannot read or write. Their other choice is to return to the hell they left, take up arms again, and try to defeat a Vietnamese army which is supplied with Soviet arms and material, and which has been hardened by two decades of combat. As if this were not enough, the Khmer Serei, even if they helped defeat the Vietnamese, would still have to contend with the former regime, the Khmer Rouge still loyal to the newly ousted premier Pol Pot and his forces. The memory of the bloody deeds of that regime is still strong and horrifying among the Khmer Serei. Perhaps the bleak prospect of the future is what has silenced many of the once happy Cambodians as much as the nightmare years they have gone through.

As it turned out, the tension we felt that day was more than our imaginations. Agence France Presse reported the following day that relief food supplies to the camp had been stopped because of what a Red Cross spokesman called the "chaotic" conditions of the camp. Emergency food supplies had been scheduled for the camp because of an attack on Camp 007; this had sent refugees pouring out of the Ban Nong Samet area and into Ban Non Mak Mun seeking a sanctuary. But now the food supplies had to be stopped, the Red Cross said, because camp residents were mobbing the trucks carrying the food supplies. "Distribution was impossible," the spokesman said, "because of the unruly behavior of the people there . . . we decided it would be unwise to take any risks.'' Red Cross officials were to meet with the same camp commander, Van Saren, who had led us on the walkthrough of the camp. Adjacent to the news item was a Reuters report that Khmer Rouge forces reported an increase in Vietnamese troops just on the other side of the border; it would bring to twenty divisions, some 200,000 men, the number of Vietnamese troops inside Cambodia. The reason for this, claimed a Khmer Rouge radio broadcast, was that the Vietnamese forces were having difficulties in quelling resistance in the guerrilla areas near the border with Thailand.

Suiaphol drove us away from Ban Non Mak Mun with a sigh of relief. We spent the night in a rustic hotel in Aranyaprathet and drove up the next morning for a look at the border area near Poipet, a village in Cambodia. We stood behind a barricade and looked across a bridge to the area occupied by Vietnamese led forces. Although we heard no gunfire, Thai military authorities reported a major clash south of Poipet that day, with tanks and heavy artillery employed. By that time we were en route forty miles inside the Thai border on the road between Aranyaprathet and Bangkok, to the camp called Sakaew.

In late 1979, Sakaew was the scene of some of the most horrible pictures to come from the Indochinese clashes. Refugee children, bloated from malnutrition, nude, sitting in puddles of water or standing forlornly in a sea of mud; old people who had become skin and bones; families dying together and being buried in mass graves—the pictures were seemingly endless, as were the refugees themselves. They walked, and in some cases crawled, across the border in various places near Aranyaprathet and eventually ended in Sakaew, which the Thais, as always, point out is a temporary holding camp. It was the plight of the people arriving in Sakaew which prompted much of the world's relief efforts. A group of U.S. Senators who visited Sakaew returned to the United States with tales of horror. (Senators who managed to get into Cambodia's once beautiful capital of Phnom Penh suggested to the government of puppet Heng Samrin that a truck route be opened from Thailand to bring supplies into the capital, which they compared roughly with the conditions of the Sakaew camp. They were turned down.) Secretary of State Cyrus Vance issued a statement which said, in part, ''I can think of no issue now before the world community and before every single nation that can lay greater claim to our concern and to our action.''

Initially there were thirty thousand refugees in Sakaew, many of them in the last stages of hunger. Field kitchens were set up, but many starved to death anyway, too far gone to be helped. Their bodies were piled in a heap at the rear of the camp, then pulled away by ox carts. They were buried in common graves close to a nearby Buddhist temple. Latrines had been dug but in the beginning seldom used because the people were too weak to get to them; they simply defecated where they were. Among the refugees then, as now, were Khmer Rouge soldiers, battle-hardened but in extremis. They had reached the limits of their endurance. In feeling pity for them, volunteer workers and relief organization crews also remembered that they were supporters of a regime which had brutalized the country and its people in efforts to turn Cambodia into a Communist state, and that the Khmer Rouge forces could be held accountable for the deaths of millions of Cambodians. The refugees hate the Vietnamese but also fear the Khmer Rouge.

In the spring of 1980, there were considerably more Khmer Rouge in evidence in Sakaew than in the other camps. Some of them were still the zombielike creatures who came out of their guerrilla bases in western Cambodia. They sat like statues, eyes downcast, trusting no one and communicating as little as possible. Some of them undoubtedly were flitting back and forth across the border, using Thailand as a sanctuary to continue their battles against the Vietnamese (again, much to the displeasure of the Thais who fear Vietnamese retaliation on their own soil). With the Khmer Rouge were families and other civilians who wore the same traumatized look and the same indifference to pain—their own or other's. The silence that we noted in the Khmer Serei camp at Ban Non Mak Mun was much in evidence in Sakaew, though for apparently different reasons. The Khmer Rouge have been taught not to make idle chatter; small children in Cambodia were taught to eavesdrop on their parents and report any suspicious conversation. Some observers at Sakaew report that the indoctrination goes on.

The camp itself is on a dry, hot, waterless plain, similar in appearance to the camp at Khao I Dang. The big question during our visit was what to do with the camp during the monsoon rains, when the dirt lanes between the huts would turn into small rivers. Thai soldiers claim the area is entirely under water during the rainy season. But for now, the camp was stretched in long, orderly rows of hut-houses. There are better-than-average facilities now in Sakaew, with adequate medical care and plenty of food. But there are constant reminders that death is not far away. As we stood talking with a group of medical personnel, a doctor suddenly burst through the group en route to the emergency ward. He was carrying a tiny bundle, a small child, and behind the doctor ran a nurse with a plastic bottle connected to the child feeding it intravenously. Both doctor and nurse looked worried. Nearby, a group of children stood in a food line waiting for stew; they looked at the scene with supreme indifference.

Now that the aid programs have moved from the makeshift to the adequate, more attention is being paid to the psychological problems of the refugees, including the boredom that seems to lie over each camp like an oppressive haze. In Sakaew the medical people have noted the remarkable lassitude of the younger people, as also observed at Khao I Dang. If there is stoicism, there is also adequate food and water. Trying to teach sanitation, basic English, and other simple skills to the refugees is the responsibility of UNHCR personnel and various volunteer agencies. Once the most tragic of the camps, Sakaew had come a long way from the first few makeshift tents, but the future of the camp in the monsoon period, as well as the future of the refugees themselves, remained an open question.

While we were in Sakaew, other events were taking place. That same day the first group of 181 refugees from camps in the northeast of Thailand left for resettlement in China. All Laotians, they were the first of 6,000 refugees the People's Republic of China agreed to take from the Thai camps, in keeping with a pledge made at the international conference on refugees in Geneva in July 1979. In keeping with that pledge, China announced it would also take 2,000 refugees each from camps in Hongkong and Malaysia. The first refugees were to be settled, said Beijing, on state farms on Hainan Island, on the south coast of China.

The Laotian refugees themselves had other ideas when, earlier, they volunteered to be resettled in China in hopes the Chinese government would organize them into an army that would drive Vietnamese troops out of Laos. Most of the Lao volunteers for China were in camps around Nong Khai, the riverport town that is the jumping-off place for travelers going from Thailand across the Mekong River into Vientiane, the administrative capital of Laos. Seven camps are located relatively close to the Mekong, which divides Thailand and Laos. The Lao volunteers said they would go to China on the chance that the Chinese, who are backing the Khmer Rouge forces in Cambodia, would be equally sympathetic to the Laotian desire to drive the Vietnamese out of Laos. At least seventeen hundred Laotians were pledged to form the nucleus of an army if China would train them. And the refugees told newsmen that at least another five thousand would follow them into China if the army became a reality. In one camp, Ban Vinai, a camp for Laotian-Meo refugees, nearly twelve thousand out of a camp population of forty thousand volunteered to resettle in China if they could be trained and equipped to fight the Vietnamese in Laos.

Again, such actions worry the Thais, who feel the Vietnamese may regard such statements as provocations and an excuse to come rolling over the Thai border. (One neutral observer in Bangkok opined that if the Vietnamese attacked Thailand at breakfast they could have lunch in Bangkok and never get off the main routes.)

At a third camp, where five thousand additional Laotians volunteered for China, one reporter said the sentiment was based on newspaper reports. The reports stated the Vietnamese were charging China with massing troops on the Laotian border in attempts to "sabotage" Laotian national security. Translated, it meant to the Laotian refugees that the Vietnamese were worried about the possibility of new attacks by China along its northern provinces. If those attacks were indeed a possibility, the Laotians wanted to be a part of them to help liberate their nation from Vietnamese rule. Sources in Bangkok felt the Chinese had little concern for the idea of a Laotian army unleashed against the Vietnamese in Laos. The real reason China launched its attacks against Vietnam in February 1979, was to punish Vietnam for its role in the overthrow of pro-Chinese Cambodian premier Pol Pot and for Vietnam's alliance with China's rival, the Soviet Union. Despite the sources, Laotian refugees at Nong Khai and Ban Vinai believe China is willing to help foment rebellion in northern Laos. The Meos believe they could handle the Laotian Communists if the Vietnamese troops were out of the way.

More than two hundred and fifty thousand Laotians have fled their country since the Communists took control of it in 1975, but the situation in Laos has gone largely unreported because of the world's attention on the boat people and the Cambodian refugees. Conditions in Laos are said to have deteriorated steadily, and the Hanoi government is tightening its hold on this once peaceful and colorful land. The Vietnamese have an estimated fifty thousand troops in Laos, and recent reports state that much of the rice crop in Laos is being used to feed the Vietnamese oppressors—an echo of the tragic situation in Cambodia, where rice was used to feed first the Khmer Rouge regime of Pol Pot, then the Vietnamese invaders through the puppet government of Heng Samrin. In confiscating the rice crops in Laos, the Vietnamese dropped all pretense of merely supporting a friendly government; it became very clear, very quickly that the Vietnamese were in charge.

Like refugees elsewhere, the Loatians consider their camps in the north of Thailand only temporary sanctuaries. And like the Cambodians, they have little regard for the Thais, a situation that also applies in reverse. The tradition of hatreds remains constant in Indochina today.

As we prepared to leave the camp at Sakaew, we took a last long look. At best, it was depressing. The thousands we looked at were homeless, held in temporary quarters. They had no real constructive activity. As in other camps, there was little privacy; sometimes sleeping quarters between a family and the one next door were defined only by a taut piece of string. The camps were noisy, making a good night's sleep a luxury. Confinement itself was nearly intolerable for people who have enjoyed the openness of country life. There was a growing number of incidents of wife beating, child abuse, and infidelity, all of which were attributed to camp life. In some camps there is a palpable fear, and with justification. At one camp, Thai camp guards allegedly murdered a refugee, and the accusation was serious enough to get an investigation underway by Thailand's Ministry of the Interior. In another camp a woman was murdered, believed killed by Thai robbers who had sneaked into the camp. In yet another camp, a woman was shot in the hand because she had talked too freely with her brother, who lived in Thailand. In most of the camps there is fear that the insurgents who operate in the area will widen the war to include the border areas of Thailand—dooming the present camps and risking a wider war involving Thai troops. And in the camps there is the sense that temporary or not, the camps may be home to thousands of refugees for a long, long time. Because processing machinery is slow, and for other reasons, boat people who have settled in other areas have been processed out of the first-settlement countries and sent on to permanent homes well ahead of the camp residents along the Thai-Cambodian border. Some of the other reasons include: Singapore's rule that no refugees be in Singapore longer than ninety days; the rule that consideration be given to refugees who have relatives in other countries or have worked closely with

U.S. agencies or units (as many of the boat people had); and the fact that other nations of Southeast Asia would not allow refugees on their soil unless they were committed to other countries and would be moved quickly. For this last reason, refugees are moved from Singapore, Malaysia, and Indonesia as quickly as possible, but they tend to languish in the camps in Thailand because there is not the urgency there as elsewhere. UNHCR officials fear that if they do not move these refugees quickly, the other Southeast Asian nations will simply stop receiving refugees under any circumstances—a policy which would doom any escapees of the future. Whatever else can be said about the traditional Thai mistrust of its neighbors, it must be admitted that Thailand, for reasons altruistic or not, has not made similar demands. Despite the 450,000 refugees in camps along its borders, Thailand did not set conditions for their speedy departure to other places. It is true that in the early days of the refugee exodus, the Thais turned back thousands of refugees. But this policy ended after consultation with the U.S. ambassador to Thailand, Morton Abramowitz.

In Suiaphol's sedan we began the drive to Bangkok, past the tapioca farms, the temples, the elephants, the water buffalo, and the farmers. We left the slash and burn agriculture of the western area, reentered the alluvial plain, and rolled by verdant farms and prosperous-looking towns. In a few hours we were back in Bangkok, a world apart from the pathos of the camps.

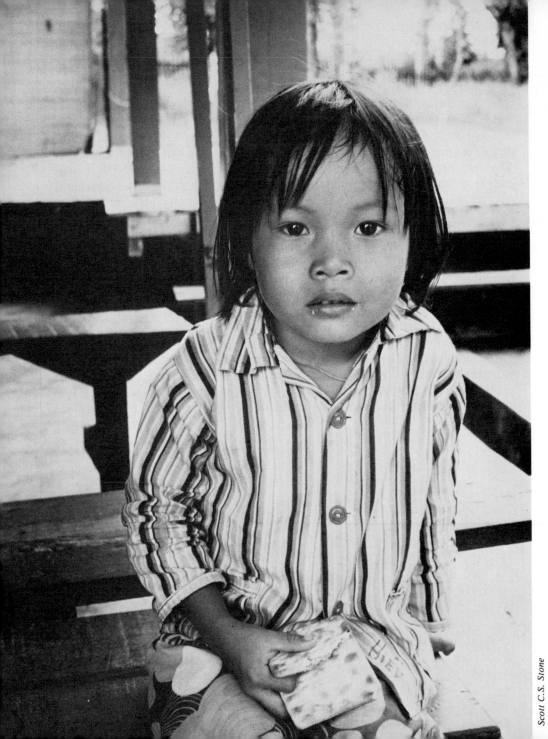

In the Hawkins Road Camp in Singapore, a winsome Chinese refugee munches crackers and awaits resettlement, probably in the United States.

Three "boat people" children take a break from English classes in the Hawkins Road Camp. They are headed for the United States

Scott C.S. Stone

Scott C.S. Stone

Two young ethnic Chinese prepare a midday meal. Within three months they will be in the United States. Hawkins Road Camp.

A small boy searches for a familiar face in Khao I Dang. More than a few children have exhibited symptoms of mental disorders because of their traumatic experiences in Cambodia, coupled with acute malnutrition.

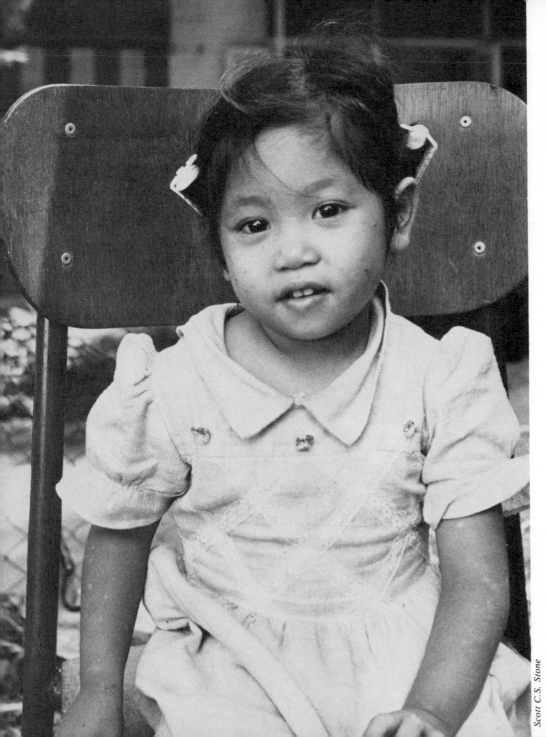

Tuyet survived a boat trip with her father and sisters. She will be resettled in Japan and start a new life, but at the moment she enjoys camp life in Singapore.

Scott C.S. Stone

A volunteer teache English to "boa people"children i the Hawkins Roa Camp in Singapore

Scott C.S. Stone

Scott C.S. Stone

Ennui afflicts many refugees in the Khao I Dang Camp along the Thai-Cambodian border. Most refugees become bored with camp life once they learn there will be sufficient food and water. Keeping them occupied is a major concern.

A Cambodian refugee child in Khao I Dang; the body is young, the eyes are old and wary.

Scott C.S. Stone

Bath time in Khao
I Dang Camp. To truck
water to this and other
border camps costs
$13,000 per day in
early 1980. Baths were
a luxury.

Scott C.S. Stone

Wood carriers walk
beside a turbid stream
on the Thai-Cambodian
border camp. Many
trees were stripped
for firewood.

In the Khao I Dang Camp this boy had the only manufactured toy seen in camp—a plastic gun.

Scott C.S. Stone

Street scene in Khao Dang Camp, the Thai Cambodian border. On of the better organized camps, Khao I Dan nevertheless suffered lack of activities and barren, desert-lik environment. Durin the day the sun coul reach 100 degrees F

Scott C.S. Stone

Cambodian men find rare amusement in a game somewhat removed from bowling. Khao I Dang Camp.

A Khmer youth ar his younger brothe Khao I Dang Cam,

Scott C.S. Stone

Scott C.S. Sto...

A Hawkins Road Camp leader (left) listens as Le Dang Khoa (right) tells how he navigated from Vietnam to Singapore in a frail boat with forty-seven aboard. Two children died en route. Le Dang Khoa will be sent on to Norway for permanent resettlement.

III

Boat People

The fall of the Saigon government on 30 April 1975 precipitated the largest emergency mass migration of refugees to the United States in our history. From April through the end of December of 1975, over 130,000 Vietnamese refugees entered the United States. In the years 1976, 1977, and 1978 an average of 1,800 per month were admitted. For the first six months of 1979, an average of 5,700 per month entered, and for the last six months of 1979 the average was 13,500.

The Vietnamese exodus, on the whole, breaks into three phases.

The first phase was the evacuation which began in April 1975, mostly of Vietnamese who had worked for U.S. government agencies in Vietnam and members of their families; these were moved out of the country by the Americans. Other evacuees of this kind were officials of the Vietnamese government who would almost certainly have been marked for elimination, imprisonment, or reeducation in the increasing likelihood of a North Vietnamese takeover.

The second phase was from mid-1975 to late 1977. In the last half of 1975, while the Communist administrators were concentrating on imposing their system in the South, escape was relatively uncomplicated. Then, in early 1976, as the authorities began to register the inhabitants in order to organize more reeducation centers and to move people from the cities to the country, more and more southerners, many of whom had fled North Vietnam in 1954, took to the boats. The available craft were small, always overcrowded, and incapable of long journeys. They headed for ports in Thailand, Malaysia, Indonesia, and Singapore. Their plight drew the world's attention to the "boat people." The hazards of the journey were more than those thrown upon them by the vagaries of the weather in the unpredictable South China Sea. Many tales of inhumanity, terror, and cruelty were reported to us.

In October 1979 a small, leaking boat plowed gamely onward in the Gulf of Thailand. The seas were choppy and the skies overcast, but the Vietnamese refugees were heartened by the thought of their imminent arrival in Thailand and safety. The refugees were a mixed lot of men, women, and children, many of them ill and most of them hungry and thirsty. One of them suddenly spotted a boat on the horizon, then another, and another. Finally, four boats came into view, and the refugees' relief turned into terror. What was about to happen to them was the thing they had dreaded most when they left Vietnam: an encounter with Thai pirates.

The pirate boats came alongside, and the Thais began towing the Vietnamese craft toward a tiny, uncharted island some fifty miles off the coast of Thailand. Once ashore, the pirates held rifles pointed at the refugees as they separated the men from the women and young girls. While some guarded the men, others took the women and girls into the bushes of the island and raped them repeatedly. Then they returned and stood guard while the other pirates took their turn in the bushes.

The terror continued for weeks, with the pirates returning to the island from time to time to hunt down the terrified females and rape them. Each time they went away, the pirates left enough food and water on the island to keep the survivors alive. One woman hid in a coastal cave and endured hundreds of crab bites rather than face the pirates. A former South Vietnamese Air Force officer, who refused to tell the pirates the hiding place of some of the women, was beaten by a hammer, hung from a tree, and finally thrown off a cliff. One terrified man revealed the hiding place of four of the women, only to be rewarded with the rape of his fifteen-year-old daughter.

On 19 November, a force of United Nations and Thai officials descended on the island having heard tales of pirate activity there. As they approached they saw corpses along the shoreline. Inland, they rounded up the traumatized women and took them, along with the surviving men, off the island and to safety.

Three weeks later a boat of Vietnamese refugees sailed close to the island, not knowing its bloody history. A pirate boat suddenly loomed nearby and closed on the refugee boat. Armed men took the women aboard and headed for the island, pausing only long enough to use a hammer and screwdriver to pry three gold teeth from one of the men; finally leaving him unconscious and with a mouth full of blood on the deck of the refugee boat. As they began the tow, the dilapidated refugee boat began to come apart, and as it settled in the water the pirates cut the tow. As the pirates watched without attempting to help and the refugee women screamed and cried, the refugee boat sank and the seventy-three men aboard it drowned. The pirate boat sailed away toward the island with the terrified women.

Again three weeks later, on New Year's Eve, three boats of refugees totaling 190 persons sailed into the Gulf of Thailand and were set upon by four pirate boats. The pirates, wielding clubs, beat some of the Vietnamese men and then ordered the survivors to swim toward the uninhabited island. Some of the women refused to head toward the island, and the pirates began throwing babies in the water until the women started to swim. By the time they had reached the island, there were only 120 of them left. The women ran away into the bushes, and the pirates followed them, hunting them down and raping them in turn. The horror continued for five days before marine forces from Thailand arrived on the island and rescued the anguished survivors. A relief organization reported that one victim, an eight-year-old girl, had been raped at least one hundred times by the pirates. As of spring 1980, there had been only fourteen arrests for piracy in Thailand and no recorded convictions.

The horror stories from the Gulf of Thailand are not the only facets of the tragedy lived by the boat people of Vietnam. By bribes or by stealth, by day and night, the Vietnamese put to sea in boats that would have made a seaman shake his head in amazement. Conditions aboard the boats were unimaginable; the idea was to put as many escapees aboard as possible, and in storms and bad seas they died by the thousands. There are no accurate figures as to the death toll of the boat people. But stories told by the survivors indicate that between 40 and 70 percent of the people who left by sea did not arrive elsewhere, victims both of a merciless ocean and the cruel regime which forced them to flee. The Vietnamese dead may total as many as four hundred thousand.

The Phase Two refugees left Vietnam for a number of reasons. There was growing discontent with the Communist overlords because economic conditions did not improve with the new leadership, they worsened. Simultaneous with the deteriorating economy was the steady erosion of personal freedoms. And many of the refugees said they were afraid of being ordered into one of the reeducation camps or into the New Economic Zones. The reeducation camps had been organized and set up by the Hanoi government. The ostensible purpose was to bring about a "change of attitude" among the southerners before they could participate in the new society. From reports reaching the West, the camps were little more than concentration camps used to punish the recalcitrant southerners, and there were tales of malnutrition, disease, and torture. The New Economic Zones were hardscrabble farms, to which thousands of urbanites with little or no experience in farming were sent. The Communists, determined to rid South Vietnam of its intellectuals and "troublemakers," banished more than a million persons to farms in the South. Because of their lack of experience, because of the proximity of another country, and because they could slip back into the cities, thousands of the workers in the New Economic Zones escaped from the drudgery of the farms.

During 1977, Vietnamese forces and the troops of Premier Pol Pot, who had ruled Cambodia since the Communists came to power in that country in 1975, fought minor skirmishes along the border of the two countries. In January 1978, Vietnam sent forces deep into Cambodia in what they claimed was a move made to subdue Cambodian terrorist activity in the Parrot's Beak area of southern Vietnam. Some of the Vietnamese troops were former soldiers of South Vietnam who had been reeducated. By Christmas Day of 1978, Cambodia and Vietnam were locked in an all-out war. Nearly a hundred thousand Vietnamese troops, along with an estimated twenty thousand antigovernment Cambodians, had control of nearly a quarter of Cambodia.

The boat people, however, faced the same initial reaction from most Southeast Asian nations, which cited economic problems, racial problems, and others for not wanting the refugees at all. An editorial in the *Asian Wall Street Journal Weekly* of 25 June 1979 took those nations and other free-world leaders to task:

> As they keep these refugees waiting, free-world leaders offer all sorts of excuses. They have economic problems at home. They are squabbling about jurisdiction. They are fretting about health hazards and worried about assimilation. Some argue that the refugees are those who lacked the backbone to defeat Communist aggression and so deserve the fate that befell them in Vietnam. Such excuses should be seen for what they are—handwringing, buckpassing and demagoguery. The refugees deserve no stigma. They have committed no crime. They are victims of totalitarianism. They are seeking freedom and a tolerable life. They are desperate. They must be helped.

Refugees continued to be turned away. In June 1979, Thai troops forced forty-two thousand Cambodians back across the border. Malaysia had refused entry to some fifty-five thousand boat people, and Indonesia had deployed a twenty-four-vessel task force to prevent the Vietnamese from reaching Indonesian soil. All cited the same pressures—economic problems in feeding and housing the refugees, fear of racial conflicts resulting from the influx of new people, and the fear of becoming involved in an armed conflict. While the last two reasons may appear xenophobic, they are very real in Asia, where the refugees of all nationalities are regarded as an expansionist movement first and a flight from oppression second. In short, many neighboring countries regard the Vietnamese exodus as a form of Vietnamese tactics, a viewpoint given impetus by the Soviet-Vietnamese friendship treaty signed in November 1978. Southeast Asian states look at the 615,000-man army under Hanoi's command and know it is one of the largest and best-equipped in the world, and capable of conventional warfare as well as guerrilla actions. At the same time, they wonder if there are Communist agents among the refugees who would strengthen Communist movements in their own countries. Thailand, in particular, views itself as being vulnerable to such actions, and it also fears that the presence of the Khmer Rouge and Khmer Serei in the refugee camps will extend the conflict into Thai territory.

By July 1979, Vietnamese refugees, most of them ethnic Chinese, were leaving their homeland at the rate of 65,000 per month. In late July, fifty nations met in Geneva for a two-day conference on this situation. The meeting was significant in that it manifested a broader recognition—and acknowledgment of the principle—that refugee assistance should be considered an international responsibility. Out of the meeting came pledges of permanent resettlement for more than 260,000 refugees and financial pledges to the United Nations High Commissioner for Refugees for the Indochina program amounting to $190 million.

Prior to Geneva, comparatively few countries were committed to a regular rate of resettlement. As a result of Geneva, the number of countries which took responsibility for resettlement and established a specific number of refugees that they would take more than doubled from the previous year. The total resettlement pledges by countries other than the United States increased substantially, from 35,970 to 123,540. Belgium, Canada, Germany, Netherlands, and Norway increased their annual quotas by 300 percent and more. In terms of the overall number of Indochinese refugees seeking a new home, these totals might not be considered significant, but the general acknowledgement on the part of the more fortunate countries of the requirement to help the refugees was significant.

Another important achievement at Geneva was the Philippine government's offer to provide the site for a facility which would serve as a refugee processing center (RPC). The United States has strongly supported the establishment of RPCs as a means of relieving the pressures on the countries of first asylum, and thereby encouraging them to continue to accept all new arrivals.

U.S. Vice President Walter Mondale proposed the establishment of an international refugee resettlement fund to provide developing countries with financing and advice needed to permanently settle refugees. The Carter administration asked Congress to appropriate $20 million for the first year provided that other nations add their own contributions for a fund which the United States recommended be capitalized at $200 million.

Then, on 16 February 1979, in an apparent move to divert the Hanoi government from its attempt to take over Cambodia, the People's Republic of China invaded Vietnam. Publicly, the Chinese stated that they were reacting to "border provocations" along the China-Vietnam frontier.

The Phase Three exodus, which started in early 1978, was, until the time of the Chinese invasion, made up of approximately equal numbers of Vietnamese and ethnic Chinese. By the end of 1978, some two months before Chinese troops crossed the Vietnamese border, about two-thirds of the refugees were ethnic Chinese citizens of Vietnam.

From the moment the North Vietnamese moved into South Vietnam in 1975, the Hanoi authorities had been applying pressure against the ethnic Chinese. In a calculated effort to get rid of the Chinese, the Communist authorities dismissed them from government jobs, applied special licensing requirements making it difficult for the merchants to conduct business, denied their children places in the schools, and subjected them to a series of other harassments.

The ethnic Chinese faced a bitter choice: leave the country in which their forebears had resided for generations—and there would be a significant departure tax—or relocate in one of the dreaded New Economic Zones and face an uncertain future. Otherwise they would be in growing confrontation with the Vietnamese Communists—more and more of them were losing their jobs or businesses; the Vietnamese schools were off limits to their children and their Chinese schools were being closed down, one by one; the quotas of Chinese assigned to detention and reeducation camps were being increased; they were subjected to a curfew; and always there was intimidation by officialdom.

More and more Chinese opted to leave. The government encouraged them to depart, but they first had to "donate" their property to the state. For those who were wavering in their decision about leaving, the Chinese invasion provided the decision for them. Hanoi formally notified their ethnic Chinese citizens that they had to leave the country. Further, they were told, in the event of "further difficulty" with the People's Republic of China, they would be imprisoned or "eliminated." While in March 1978 the average monthly number of persons leaving was two thousand, in April an estimated fifty thousand boat people got out of the country.

As no transportation was provided by the Vietnamese government, the refugees were forced to leave in any vessel they could find. The boats were always overcrowded and often unseaworthy. One U.S. official estimated that between thirty thousand and fifty thousand persons drowned each month from May through July 1979.

The price of departure was high, about two thousand dollars per person; it was paid to Vietnamese officials and gold was preferred. To help some of them get out, relatives among overseas Chinese began to contribute, and in 1979 alone remitted several hundred million dollars to the Bank of Vietnam. In late 1979, international banking sources in Hongkong estimated the moneys accruing to the Vietnamese government for the release of the Chinese refugees averaged about $90 million per month. Thus the Hanoi government was doubly glad to see the Chinese choose to leave—they had become a satisfactory export item, and their exodus rid the country of a group the Vietnamese wanted out for a number of reasons. The Chinese, or Vietnamese of Chinese origin, had played a leading role in the country's economy for a long time. When Hanoi ordered the elimination of private commerce (including the confiscation of thirty thousand private businesses in South Vietnam in March 1978), it was a blow to the Chinese businessmen. So was the amalgamation in May 1978, of the two currencies used in North and South Vietnam since 1975. At the same time, there were developing racial conflicts because the Communists questioned the loyalty of the Chinese in the event of a war between Vietnam and the People's Republic of China.

At two separate conferences sponsored by the United Nations—one in December 1978, at the United Nations and one in Jakarta in May 1979—several delegations accused the Hanoi government of a cynical exportation of people in order to raise gold and currency it could not raise in other ways. There was some justification in the charge. The new masters in South Vietnam were unable to cope with the economic problems, which were due largely to poor management and natural disasters. In the fall of 1978, Vietnam suffered one of the worst seasons in its recorded history, being savaged in turn by droughts, typhoons, cold waves, and flooding. Additionally, there was a shortage of fertilizer, insecticides, and farming tools and equipment. These problems, coupled with the resistance of farmers to the nationalization of their land, made it necessary for Vietnam to import two million tons of rice into what was once one of the richest rice-growing regions of the world. Not helping the situation were the 1978 border clashes with China and the Christmas Day invasion of Cambodia. The seventeen-day strike by the Chinese forces into Vietnam diverted army units which might otherwise have been involved in reconstruction efforts, and analysts in 1980 were saying that the number of Vietnamese troops on the China-Vietnam border had increased from 70,000 to 200,000. Similarly, the armed forces tied up with Khmer guerrillas in western Cambodia initially involved 125,000 men but increased by 1980 to at least 180,000. With little military manpower available for reconstruction, a scarcity of everything else, and a sure money crop in its ethnic Chinese, the Hanoi government seized its opportunity.

To the consternation of the escaping boat people, and to much of the world as well, the escapees were not greeted with open arms. In November 1978, two rusting freighters, the *Hai Hong* and the *Southern Cross,* sailed onto the world scene and heralded the increase in refugees the world could expect. Despite the fact that there was a terrible immorality in Hanoi's expulsion of its own people as an economic activity, there was a reluctance in some areas to accept the refugees—or at least a loud outcry at the prospects of unwanted new people.

In Malaysia, Deputy Prime Minister Mahathir Mohamad issued inflammatory statements to the effect that the boat people would be expelled, that they would be drowned if they tried to sink their boats in Malaysian waters in hope of rescue, that he would seek legislation enabling Malaysia to shoot on sight any additional refugees trying to come ashore. Mahathir's outburst was discounted by other Malaysian officials, however, and by February 1979, there were 50,897 refugees in Malaysian camps at Pulau Tengah, Pulau Besar, Pulau Bidong, Kota Baru, Kuatan, Sabah, Sarawak, and a transit center. By the following June there were about 74,000 refugees, and by early 1980 the United States had pledged to take some 3,000 per month out of Malaysia. For all its unpromising beginnings, the refugee situation in Malaysia was on its way and working out as well as most. But the initial storm over the refugees' arrival cost Malaysia dearly in terms of world image.

The refugees in Malaysia received rice, meat, vegetables, and fish, and most camps had sufficient food. The camp at Pulau Bidong was marked by chaotic conditions due in part to the monsoons which disrupted distribution of food supplies. There were difficulties with the Malaysian government as well; the UNHCR wanted time to prepare the facilities, but in August 1978, the camp opened in a near crisis atmosphere, with twenty-five thousand refugees crowding the camp. New arrivals had problems because food was ordered for the estimated number of people in the camp, but the rapid influx of new refugees put foodstuffs in short supply. The most recent arrivals were forced to buy food from the black market, share the small rations of the older camp residents, or go hungry. At Pulau Bidong there were only two wells for fresh water, with other wells started without solid support and quickly turning into mudholes; from these people drank. There were more than a dozen cases of infectious hepatitis.

In Singapore (see Chapter VI), the refugees' condition was nearly idyllic by comparison with other camps. Conditions were also good in Indonesia where there were refugee camps, at Tinjang Pinjang in the Riau archipelago near Singapore, and in Jakarta suburbs. In Southeast Asian countries, the boat people had one significant advantage over the land refugees in Thailand: they were processed and sent on their way in a faster, more orderly manner. While the land refugees were in camps at least a year and in some cases longer, the boat people were processed in a matter of months. Although their voyages were filled with the worst kind of hazards, their eventual journey to a permanent home was virtually assured once they reached the Philippines, Malaysia, Singapore, Indonesia, or Hongkong.

At the Geneva meeting the United States also outlined its decision to instruct the U.S. Seventh Fleet to expand its efforts to locate and rescue boat people in distress in the South China Sea. Long-range Navy P-3 reconnaissance aircraft were ordered to search for refugees in distress and to alert ships in the area as to their whereabouts. By this time, however, the Vietnamese government had put into effect a moratorium on refugee boat departures which resulted in a marked decline in the number of boat refugees. The Navy's search and rescue operations nevertheless resulted in the rescue of approximately seven hundred boat refugees.

At Geneva, Vietnam, in referring to its agreement with the U.N. High Commissioner for Refugees, said that "orderly departure" would be guaranteed. At this writing it is too early to speculate whether that promise will be kept. In March 1980, a Japanese journalist reported from Vietnam that the government is determined to carry out a "population purge" of persons unable or unwilling to "adapt" to socialism. Thus it is possible that more boat people may be created.

The Vietnamese agreement with the U.N. High Commissioner for Refugees was reached in May 1979 (See Appendix 2). Under the terms of this agreement, Vietnam will permit the departure of Vietnamese citizens who wish to leave the country to join relatives abroad or to work. Although people of this category would not be refugees in the accepted sense of the word, the UNHCR undertook to facilitate departures by coordinating resettlement in recipient countries. Under the terms of the agreement, the

Vietnamese authorities and the recipient countries will prepare lists of those permitted to leave and those accepted for resettlement. Those appearing on both lists will be qualified for exit from Vietnam. Those not on both lists are to be the subject of further discussion.

The United States is cooperating with the UNHCR concerning individuals who would qualify for entry into the United States. The American Embassy in Bangkok set up a special processing unit to facilitate the work of reuniting American citizens and permanent residents with qualified residents who are still living in Vietnam. The first of the lists was provided to the UNHCR in May 1979, with subsequent lists following as additional petitions were received and processed. While the United States has not made funds available to pay for travel to America for those Vietnamese who receive exit permits, the Inter-Governmental Committee on European Migration will provide travel loans to petitioners in the United States.

While the half million Vietnamese boat people were occupying the attention of the non-Communist world, another mass of refugees from North Vietnam were crossing the border into the People's Republic of China. In mid-September 1979, Beijing appealed to the U.N. High Commissioner for Refugees for financial aid to help resettle the Vietnamese refugees in the People's Republic of China. The Chinese also asked the UNHCR to process the applications of those who qualify for further emigration to other countries.

According to the Chinese, a total of 221,000 refugees have been resettled on state farms: 78,000 in Guangxi Province, 27,000 in Yunnan, and 116,000 in Guangdong and Fujian provinces. Another 30,000 were in temporary camps along the Vietnamese border.

Many of these refugees consider China to be a stopping point on the way to what they hope will be permanent homes in Canada, the United States, Australia, or France. Many of the ethnic Chinese refugees from North Vietnam were educated in schools established by the French and are aware that the French have a special sympathy for the people of Vietnam.

The United States, too, has a special sympathy for the Vietnamese, but for different reasons. Our country has been particularly generous in the financial aid allotted to Indochinese refugees. In addition to the contributions made to the international agencies, the United States has, through a number of domestic programs, provided additional assistance to the refugees who have settled here.

In April 1975, President Ford made available $100 million in U.S. Agency for International Development funds for assistance to Indochinese refugees. Shortly thereafter, the Indochina Migration and Refugee Assistance Act of 1975 was enacted. This legislation authorized assistance to or on behalf of Indochinese refugees under the terms of the Migration and Refugee Assistance Act of 1962. Assistance to refugees living in the United States was initially authorized through 30 September 1977, then extended. There are also activities funded through the Department of Health, Education and Welfare budget under the Indochinese refugee program. These include reimbursing states for cash assistance, medical assistance, and social services provided to needy refugees, and for the operation of English language and employment training projects.

The Indochina Refugee Children Assistance Act of 1976 authorized assistance to local educational agencies for services to Indochinese refugee children and to state and local educational agencies for adult refugee education activities. This legislation was amended to authorize assistance to the local agencies for the education of Indochinese refugee children who entered the United States after 1 January 1977. It covers fiscal years through 1981. These amendments also authorize assistance for adult education programs for Indochinese refugees for fiscal years 1979 through 1983.

IV

Vietnamese Exodus

The saga of the Vietnamese boat people of the late 1970s is not unique. In 1954, nearly a million Vietnamese fled communist-controlled North Vietnam to come south across the dividing line of the 17th Parallel. The great majority came by boat—in rafts across the Ben Hai River, in frail fishing vessels, in sturdy U.S. Navy landing craft, in chartered cargo ships, in virtually any craft that would float, seaworthy or not, down the South China Sea to South Vietnam.

The Geneva Accords, a result of the international conference on the Far East, guaranteed the civilian population the right to move to either zone. They were "to be assisted in doing so" by the authorities in both zones. But the assistance was all one-sided. Some 140,000 persons who had been living in the South applied to the authorities to go to the North. The South Vietnamese government arranged their transportation promptly. The reverse movement was a different story. Two days after the terms of the accords were announced, the North Vietnamese Communists, the Viet Minh, launched a propaganda campaign against the French, Americans, and South Vietnamese. Simultaneously, all young men and women were ordered to attend "reeducation" classes for three hours every morning, where the political commissars told them of barbarities perpetrated by the Americans, French, and South Vietnamese.

A key clause in the accords provided that a crescent-shaped area around Haiphong, 40 miles from Hanoi and its seaport, was to remain an "open zone to both parties." The area around Hanoi and the corridor from Hanoi to Haiphong, which contained a highway and a railroad, were to be patrolled by French Union troops, and were also to remain "open and free" until 19 May 1955. Those areas were to be the staging points for northerners who wished to move to South Vietnam. The area around Hanoi was to contract gradually until 18 May 1955, the final date for evacuation, when the city would come under control of the communists.

But on 22 July the Viet Minh began to block the open zones so that persons desiring to move south could not get through. While in the beginning the Viet Minh did not enter the open zones, which were patrolled by French Union forces, nighttime hit-and-run raids were common. Viet Minh guerrillas and regular troops murdered or maimed hundreds whom they suspected of wanting to go south. Homes were looted and burned.

Despite all the difficulties and harassments between 21 July 1954 and 18 May 1955, more than 860,000 refugees managed to get to the free South. Estimates of those who wished to leave but were blocked by the Viet Minh range from 250,000 to 500,000. These estimates were based on statements of those who managed to get to the South and told of relatives who desired to flee but were prevented from doing so.

The story of the movement of the refugees from North to South Vietnam is one which has been recounted in print many times and need not be repeated here. The year 1955 did not see the end of the struggle between North and South Vietnam. It was to continue for another twenty years, until, in 1975, the South Vietnamese government collapsed under the onslaught of North Vietnamese troops. The second wave of boat people was to begin in April of that year.

At the same time the American ambassador in Saigon was steadfastly claiming that there was no danger to the city—no doubt on instructions from the State Department in Washington—but air evacuation of key Vietnamese who had worked for the Americans, their families, Vietnamese wives and children of Americans, and families of Vietnamese government officials, was underway. These early refugees were carried out on the U.S. C-141 and C-130 transports which were flying in emergency military supplies in the hope of bolstering the defense of Saigon. The flights, which began on 5 April 1975, took the refugees to Clark Air Force Base in the Philippines.

Then, on 23 April, six days before the final American evacuation of Saigon, a fleet of additional planes was called into service and began to take Vietnamese refugees to the island of Guam. Some twenty-five hundred persons a day were brought to Andersen Air Force Base and the U.S. Naval Air Station on Guam. Under the optimistic name Operation New Life, American military and civilian employees organized a reception center on Guam for the refugees. By 29 April, when the last exodus of Americans from Saigon was effected, the refugees on Guam numbered more than twenty-five thousand. Although military and commercial planes were transporting the Vietnamese from Guam to the United States at the average rate of one thousand a day, the arrivals far exceeded the departures.

On 7 May, American and Vietnamese cargo vessels, U.S. and Vietnamese Navy craft, and a few small Vietnamese ships, arrived with more evacuees. By 14 May, there were more than fifty thousand refugees on the island.

During all of this time U.S. Navy Seabees and an American commercial construction firm worked around the clock to provide quarters for the refugees. Tents were erected, buildings were constructed, water pipes were laid, electricity and telephone wires appeared—all at a breathtaking pace. Plywood huts were set up and field kitchens put in place. A Guamanian company made deliveries twenty-four hours a day of pipes, fittings, and necessary hardware. The government of Guam assigned a fleet of buses to the operation. A ship from Taiwan delivered twenty-five hundred tons of rice. On 28 April, the U.S. Army's 45th Support Group arrived and took over administration of the main camp at Orote Point. The American Red Cross, the International Rescue Committee, the Intergovernmental Committee for European Migration (ICEM), the Office of the U.N. High Commissioner for Refugees (UNHCR), Catholic Relief Services, and other voluntary organizations sent in teams to help process the refugees. The Guam Visitors Bureau recruited volunteers to help with camp nurseries, clothing collection, and other services. Families on Guam would come to the camp and take refugees to their homes for a meal. Schools and churches helped in many other ways. Military chaplains, local clergy, and visiting missionaries worked alongside Vietnamese priests, monks, and nuns. The local radio and TV station dedicated several hours a day to Vietnamese language broadcasts. A Vietnamese language newspaper was published daily. The Guam Federation of Teachers and the Kiwanis Club of Guam organized English language classes.

By mid-September more than ninety-two thousand refugees who were quartered on Guam had been resettled. Some eighty-six thousand went to the United States and the remainder to fourteen other countries. Today the camps are empty, largely dismantled, their sites a reminder of the resolution, organization, and efficiency humans are capable of when their sympathies are touched.

The story of the rout that occurred when the Americans left Saigon in 1975, and the pictures of helicopters leaving the roof of the American Embassy are still vivid in the minds of many Americans. The stories of individual bravery—and cowardice—have been recounted. The imaginative feats of many, Americans as well as Vietnamese, evoked admiration and sometimes awe.

One person who will long be remembered for his brave exploits in the dying days of Vietnam is Edward Joseph Daly, president of World Airways. In 1975, World Airways was a nonscheduled airline engaged in flying contract missions between the United States and Vietnam. Daly's charter firm flew many mercy missions in and out of Da Nang when that city was surrounded by North Vietnamese troops. Similarly, his planes shuttled in and out of Saigon. In the first week of April 1975, Daly was in Saigon attempting to obtain clearance to fly fifty-seven orphaned Vietnamese children to their new homes in the United States. The local adoption agency, Friends for All Children, the U.S. consulate, and Daly were snarled in red tape. As the confusion heightened the 52-year-old Daly, a former boxer and Army Air Corps staff sergeant, got tougher than usual. Certain that it was only a matter of days before Saigon would fall, he decided to fly the fifty-seven orphans without clearances. He assembled the young Vietnamese —some were abandoned children of American GIs—and got them to Tan Son Nhut Airport in Saigon. He put the children, along with their escorts, on one of his airline's DC-8s at the far end of one of the runways. Daly ordered his pilot to taxi to the end of the runway preparatory to taking off. The air traffic controller at the busy airport became frantic. "Don't take off. Do not, repeat, do not take off. You have no clearance." The pilot, Ken Healy, looked at Daly for instructions. "Go," said Daly. The pilot gunned the four jet engines, and the plane sped down the runway and lifted off to the screaming threats of the air traffic controller. Aboard, the plane was a flying picnic ground. Daly had stocked the aircraft with bananas, crackers, milk, sandwiches, rice, and the fish sauce which the Vietnamese use as Americans use ketchup and mustard. There were a few toys, packs of crayons, and sketch pads. The twenty adult supervisors played games with the youngsters when they weren't changing the babies' diapers—a supply of which Daly had somehow managed to acquire. During the night hours of the flight, the orphans slept peacefully, cuddled in blankets. The plane flew nonstop to Oakland, California where it touched down smoothly on the airport runway. This was the first of many to arrive. News of the plane's departure had been flashed from Saigon. More than five hundred people who had been awaiting its arrival broke into a cheer. As the children, whose ages ranged from two months to thirteen years, came off the plane, the eyes of most of the spectators welled with tears. A dozen families approached the twenty adult escorts and asked if they could adopt children on the spot.

Ed Daly's first group of youngsters was taken by bus from Oakland to the Presidio of San Francisco, an army post in the shade of the Golden Gate Bridge. Here, feverish preparations for their arrival had consumed two days as the Presidio's commander and his staff worked to transform a rather sleepy base into the largest pediatric ward in medical history.

On the Presidio end, it all had started on a Tuesday at about noon when Daly's daughter, Charlotte, called the Presidio commander to ask if he could accomodate the already airborne children that her father was bringing from Saigon. She said that they would arrive Thursday night and, further, nobody else could or would help her. Sticking his neck way out, he agreed, putting down one telephone while picking up another to notify his parent headquarters of his intentions.

The first place selected to house the children was the Presidio Reserve Center, a large armorylike building with extensive concrete floors. On these, Presidio soldiers placed GI mattresses, enough for about 150 children and volunteer escorts. Army cooks set up a kitchen in an anteroom, and the military police secured the doors. While supplies and equipment were being assembled, hundreds of volunteers from the San Francisco Bay Area were put on schedules for meeting planes and acting as escorts. Physicians, civilian and military, joined forces with nurses and paramedics to conduct physical examinations and treat those who arrived sick.

The plan, developed jointly with Friends For All Children and many other similar agencies, was to have the children stay at the Presidio for only twenty-four hours to be processed to their adoptive families. It did not work out that way, unfortunately, since some of the children had to stay at the Presidio for ten days or more. They simply came too fast to permit an orderly assimilation into the adoption machinery.

After Daly's first few planeloads of children, the U.S. Air Force took over, delivering the orphans from Saigon to the United States. Most of these planes came through Manila to land at Travis Air Force Base, but toward the end of Orphan Airlift, several such flights were diverted to both the Los Angeles and Seattle areas where centers similar to that of the Presidio were established to process orphans.

In all, some fifteen hundred children went through the Presidio for eventual adoption throughout the United States and to countries such as France and Sweden. The great majority were sick with a variety of ailments when they arrived, but they were successfully treated by the skilled medical people who gave so unstintingly of their time. After the first few days, the entire medical effort was under the direct supervision of Letterman Army Medical Center which amalgamated the volunteer physicians and nurses with its own personnel to provide the care so badly needed.

There was only one casualty among the children—a very young baby, from an advanced ear infection which existed prior to her leaving Saigon— which attests to the high degree of professionalism established by all people on duty at the center. During the month that the centers were open, all pediatric wards in San Francisco and environs were filled with the more seriously ill children. Most, however, remained at the refugee center at the Presidio, receiving treatment from the physicians on duty there.

This tremendous humanitarian exercise provided insights into the treatment of mass casualties such as might occur in a nuclear war. Never before had so many sick children been assembled for treatment in such a short time and at one place. Even in the course of the most difficult conditions of a modern battlefield, the numbers of persons evacuated and treated would come to only a percentage of the numbers processed through the Presidio and other centers in April 1975. Similar procedures adopted in time can help alleviate much suffering and save many lives if some catastrophic occurrence makes such action necessary.

But not all the orphan lifts from Saigon had a happy ending. The first Air Force plane in the airlift, a huge C5-A Galaxy, the biggest aircraft in the world, took off with 243 orphans aboard. Minutes after takeoff the rear cargo loading door blew out and the cabin pressure dropped dangerously. With the orphans short of oxygen—there were insufficient oxygen masks for all the passengers—the pilot turned back to Saigon. The plane crash-landed in a field three kilometers from the airport. One hundred and fifty-one of the orphans and fifty adults were killed. The survivors came to the Presidio on a subsequent flight.

For these boat people awaiting immigration registration and space in a refugee camp, life goes on as usual. Food and water are provided by the Hong-kong government but distribution remains a problem in the overcrowded conditions on board.

*For the luckiones, rescue at sea b
large freighters mea
safety and a spee
journey, but still
cramped condition*

Specially designed living huts have been constructed at the many refugee camps, providing space, electric light and fans, and cover. These refugees are seen outside one of the new huts, under the clothes-drying roof.

Shade from the burni
sun is always diffic
to find at sea, even
the larger ship

Space at the
Government Dockyard
Transit Camp is limited,
but there is cover, light,
protection, and the
opportunity to catch
up on lost sleep for
these refugees waiting
to move on to other
refugee camps.

Waiting to move o
from the Governmen
Dockyard Transit Cam
means washing, eating
a stroll in the fresh ai
staring in wonder at th
Hongkong skyline, o
just looking for familia
faces among thos
waiting to land from th
many small boats tha
arrive each day

'tanding or sitting room
nly for those crammed
nto the smaller boats,
ut they still risk their
'ves on the open sea on
ourneys of over 1000
iiles sometimes lasting
everal weeks.

Young faces reflect
the happiness of
freedom, curiosity and
shyness with a stranger,
the doubt and worry
over whatever future
the world may offer,
wherever it may be.

Government of Hong Kong Information Services

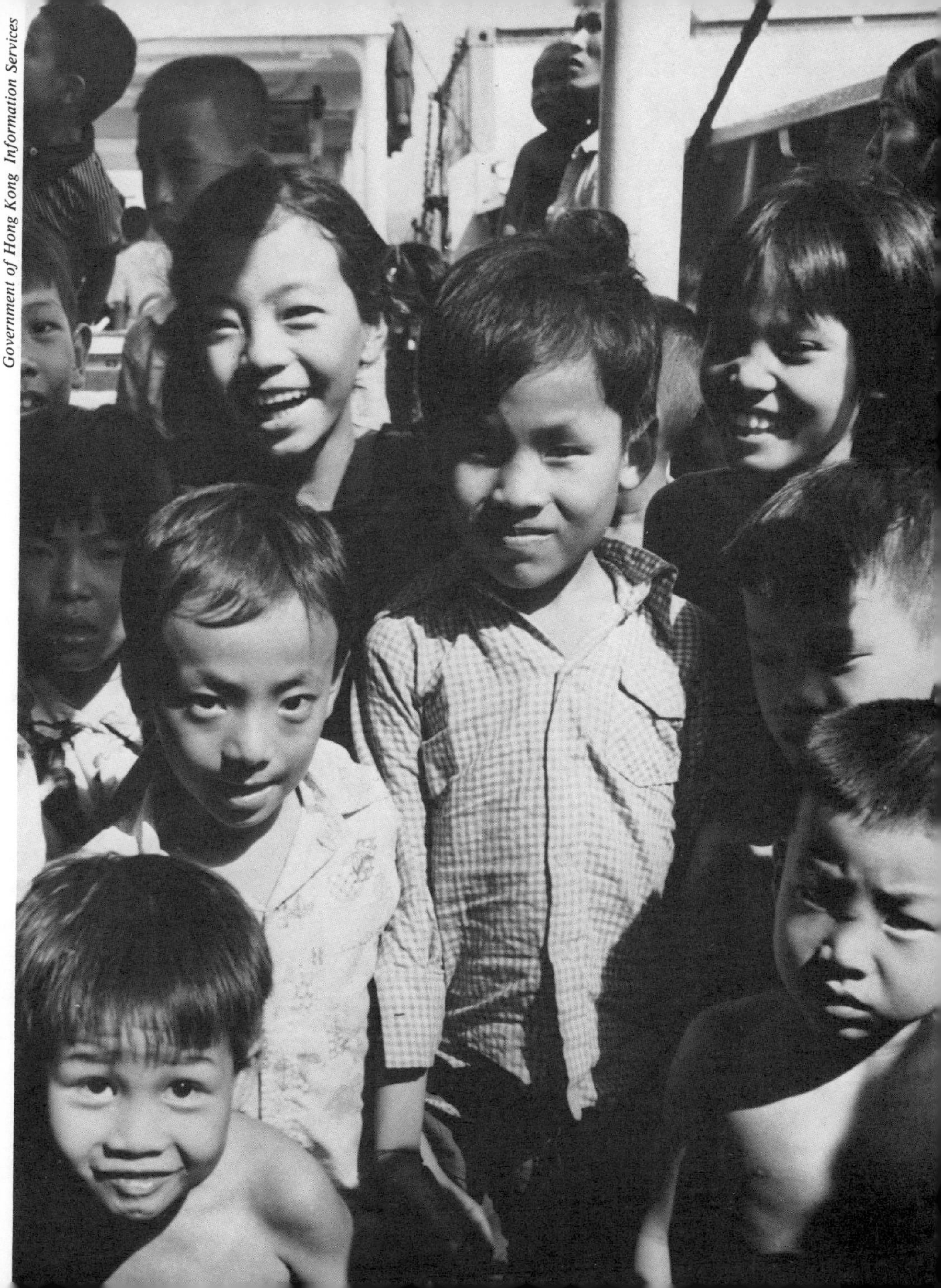

South China Sea . . . Vietnamese refugee child draws a picture on paper provided by the crew of the replenishment oiler, USS Wabash, AOR-5. The refugee children were picked up from small boats along with adult Vietnamese refugees.

Official Navy Photograph PH3 Mathew Broadway, photographer

Even bab
are fingerprint
Identification is
important part
documentation
arrival at the refu
camps. The family h
is being assisted
volunteer members
the Civil Aid Serv

The horror of past life is replaced by foreboding of an unknown future life.

A navy man on board the combat store ship USS White Plains, AFS-4, tries to entertain Vietnamese refugee children picked up from small boats in the South China Sea.

Vietnamese refugees from the combat store ship USS White Plains, *AFS-4.*
The ship picked them up from small boats in the South China Sea.

V

Hongkong

Long before the boat people sought haven in Hongkong, the lively, commercial, colorful—but densely packed—British Crown Colony on the southeast coast of China had its refugee problem.

For decades Hongkong had taken in thousands of refugees from the People's Republic of China and was hampered by shortages of housing and by strained social services. It has a total area of four hundred square miles but the majority of its population of 4.9 million lives in less than ninety square miles of urban area crowded between the hillsides and the magnificent harbor. By the end of 1978, there were more than two million people in public housing, and the housing authority had plans to provide low rent housing for another one and a half million people by 1986. Nevertheless, housing and crowding remained a problem.

Those Chinese who came south to cross into Hongkong without papers were considered illegal immigrants. Only when they were actually apprehended crossing the border would they be turned back by the Hongkong authorities. Once in the Colony, they were permitted to stay. But this tolerant attitude was coupled with the concern that the "I-Is," the illegal immigrants, would continue to flood Hongkong and make living standards intolerable. In 1979, there were 89,241 illegal immigrants in Hongkong and 94,557 legal ones. On 15 January 1980, Commercial Radio in Hongkong told its early morning listeners that the British garrison there would be boosted by one thousand men to help turn back the illegal immigrants, raising the total of troops engaged in this effort to nine thousand. The new troops would be from the 1st Battalion of the Parachute Regiment, a special raiding section of the Royal Marines, and two companies of Gurkhas. Despite the crowding and the extra troops, when the boat people began arriving in Hongkong they were not turned away. And they arrived in numbers: from 1975 through the end of 1979, 85,326 boat people made their way to Hongkong, where government sources estimated that about half of those who began the trip lived to reach safety. Of the ones who did make it, 85 percent were ethnic Chinese. Nearly 70 percent of them arrived in small boats from seaports in North Vietnam, and about 20 percent sailed from central and southern Vietnam. Another 10 percent were dispatched from Vietnam in government-organized vessels and about two percent were rescued at sea. By far the greatest number of boat people reached Hongkong in 1979—73,692 of them. From 1975 to 1979, just over 30,000 of the refugees had been settled elsewhere, with about one-third of them going to the United States.

By January 1980, there were some fifty-five thousand Indochinese refugees in camps in Hongkong, and they were adding to the responsibilities of the already overburdened social services of the Colony. Areas earmarked for industrial development were used to provide housing for the refugees, and the scheduled development programs had to be delayed. Additionally, there seemed no way to hasten the resettlement operations. While some eight thousand refugees per month were being taken from Malaysia, the United Nations quota for moving the refugees to places of final asylum was only four hundred per month. The government had originally estimated that Hongkong would still be sheltering forty-five thousand refugees by the end of 1979, barring new arrivals, but the total was ten thousand higher because the boat people continued to come. The resettlement operation did speed up in the first two months of 1980 and at the beginning of March 1980, the number was down to forty-eight thousand.

There were four camps in Hongkong—Sham Shui Po, Jubilee, and Kai Tak North and Kai Tak East near Kai Tak Airport. On a cold, blustery day in January 1980, we visited the camp at Kai Tak East, and the following day, equally cold, we went out to Sham Shui Po to talk with refugees. Both camps were on the Kowloon side, opposite Victoria Island, the main island of Hongkong.

At Kai Tak East we were escorted by Cheng Puck Fong, who works for a charitable organization in Hongkong called Caritas, which has been assisting the refugees. He told us that 75 percent of the refugees in the camp were Cantonese, that 15 percent of them were Catholics, and the rest Buddhists. On a walk about the camp we saw modern housing units, temporary but strong and serviceable; these had been provided by the government of the Federal Republic of Germany at a cost of a million dollars. There were twenty-five housing units, each containing about four hundred refugees. Since the camp had opened in June 1979, there had been sixteen deaths and 223 births. Of the roughly nine thousand people in the camp, at least three thousand of them were children.

And they were everywhere. Adequately dressed and well-fed, the children were out in the cold weather, chasing each other and playing games. They lined up for the photos taken for the immigration forms which would eventually lead to their resettlement elsewhere, far from Vietnam. They crowded around a pretty Chinese newscaster doing a spot for a television program, and they also went to school. We visited classrooms where the children were learning English. There were the usual pictures of animals and pets, a cutout of a large dog, and a picture of Bambi. When we told one of the volunteer teachers that children in other refugee camps were showing symptoms of psychological problems, she was not surprised:

> At first these children drew a few pictures of bombs going off, and of boats. We didn't encourage that, of course. Now they draw pictures of their families and camp life. We encourage them to take the pictures home with them and talk about them with their parents. It may help dispel some of the old fears, and it may bring the families closer. At least it's worth the effort.

She also noted that when the children first arrived in camp they fought with each other to get to the head of the line for food and other amenities. Now, she said, they seemed confident they would be taken care of and were more polite. Some of the children apparently had a few bad dreams initially, but the mental health of the children was not a major concern in this camp.

Cheng Puck Fong told us that many of the refugees had been able to find jobs, mostly in construction, and were earning a salary. He put the figure as high as four thousand in the labor force. Some of the refugees still had gold they brought with them and were able to buy goods beyond those provided by the camp itself. Consequently, many of the refugees are self-supporting and some of them, Cheng Puck Fong said, live better than the Hongkong residents nearby. The camp itself was spacious, clean, and afforded more shelter and privacy than any of the camps on the Thai-Cambodian border. They were also far less crowded.

In Kai Tak East we learned about the mechanics of getting out of Vietnam. Two special offices were created by the Vietnamese government early in 1978 especially for this program. One was in Haiphong in the north, one in Ho Chi Minh City in the south. There were subordinate offices in areas with large ethnic Chinese populations. After they were organized, the special offices were moved out of government buildings into private quarters to maintain the fiction that the government was not involved. But the administration of the program continued with the Public Security Bureau, the political police of the Vietnamese government. The bureau itself certifies the passenger list and collects the fees, then sets the departure date. Occasionally, Public Security Bureau officials themselves arrange for purchase and repair of boats. The entire process once took six months, but more recently the bureau was managing it in about a month. There are also middlemen, usually ethnic Chinese former businessmen who lost their positions with the fall of the Saigon government in 1975. The middlemen often arrange departures of a number of boats before leaving themselves. The middleman enlists passengers, collects the fees, negotiates an exit tax with the Public Security Bureau, and finds the boat. Since the boat often needs repairs and repair items are scarce, the middleman must buy materials from the Public Security Bureau itself. Then the middleman must provide a chart, compass, fuel, and supplies—again in short supply, but available through the black market.

Then we learned of one man's harrowing experience. He is a young man with basic English, and with the assistance of Cheng Puck Fong, he told this story:

We lived in a little village near Nha Trang. My father is dead. There was my wife, my sister and my mother—we were the ones who decided to come out. We left behind five brothers and four sisters.

We told the government we wanted to leave, and our names were placed on a list. The list was sent to the security police, who checked us out for subversive activities.

Our price for getting out was eight ounces of gold for each adult and three to four ounces per child. Young children were allowed to go free.

So we left in a boat after going through all the procedures. We sailed on July 9, 1979, and almost immediately ran into a heavy storm. It was so bad it was unbelievable. There were 272 people on the boat, a boat about fifty feet by twelve feet. We were almost swamped, so everyone took turns bailing, an hour at a time. It went on for three days, a tremendous storm. Then in the middle of the night we ran up on a sandy beach. We had no idea where we were. The next morning we found out—we were still in Vietnam, down on the southern coast in a little town. The boat was badly damaged.

We stayed in the village schoolhouse for two weeks. The government sent us by cars and buses back to Nha Trang, and we didn't know then what was going to happen. We were afraid of the storms, but we wanted to leave. We didn't know if the government would charge us more to get out the second time. But they simply gave us another boat, the same size as the first one but with more people on it, and sent us off again.

After two days at sea the motor failed, and we began to drift. Finally we ran up on a beach once again, and again we didn't know where we were. Finally we got the motor going again and finally made it into Hongkong. I am hoping to go on to the United States.

Other sources detailed the relentless exploitation of the Chinese. Having declared their intention to leave, many Chinese immediately lost their jobs and some lost their ration cards or had their rations reduced. They had to forfeit their personal property or sell it quickly. The price of departure did not include a safe-conduct pass, and guards at checkpoints had to be bribed.

At the embarkation points, the refugees were held in camps until the Public Security Bureau approved their departure; to exist in the camps the refugees had to draw on their own funds and resources. As soon as the refugees were at sea, the Vietnamese government declared them in a kind of nonperson status, meaning that if they ran into Vietnamese coastal patrol boats, they had to pay an additional bribe to sail on to the open sea. Large boats cost as much as $180,000, not including fuel and supplies, and in some cases the Public Security Bureau collected a portion of the purchase price of the boats, perhaps as much as 40 percent. In payment, the government wanted gold. *The Far East Economic Review,* that authoritative and readable journal, estimated that in 1978 the Vietnamese government made $115 million from refugee taxes. That was approximately equal to Hanoi's annual hard currency export earnings or to its known official foreign exchange holdings.

The strained conditions in the holding camps were described by a young woman in the Kai Tak East camp. With her husband and small daughter, they waited in a camp for twenty days before being herded aboard a boat.

> We paid eight ounces of gold for each of us, but they let my small daughter go free. We both left our parents in Ho Chi Minh City. In the camp we had little food and water. By selling our gold watches, we were able to buy some rice and soup and flour. Once on the boat we went through several storms—it was terrifying. But we reached Hongkong in April (1979), and we hope to resettle somewhere permanently. My husband is an electrician. Maybe we will go to the United States.

The next day at the Sham Shui Po transit center, we found James K. Reid, a Glasgow Scot who had been with the RAF, the Royal Engineers, seconded to British Intelligence, and who was now a longtime civilian in Hongkong. With long experience in hospital administration, he was now the center manager of the Sham Shui Po camp. The camp featured the same excellent housing areas and the same laughing children we saw at Kai Tak East, and Reid had a long list of visitors who had seen the camp and went away impressed. A feature of the camp was a newspaper published in Chinese, Vietnamese, and English. Called *Hope,* the newspaper carried articles on refugee problems and situations, including tips on what to expect in various stages of departure. One special edition titled the "International Year of the Child" outlined the situation of the children in the Hongkong camps, citing the skin infections, lack of vitamins, and lack of proper weight as continuing problems—still conditions were better than earlier, when children were bloated with starvation. Other editions of the newspaper carried feature articles on the countries which were accepting refugees.

Much of the organization and administration of the Hongkong camps paralleled the Hawkins Road camp in Singapore which we later visited. Both camps were far removed from the conditions on the Thai-Cambodian border. Additionally, residents of the Singapore camp could count on resettlement in three or four months. By contrast, the processing machinery on the Thai-Cambodian border was not functioning very well at the end of 1979, possibly because there was common knowledge that the camps would continue to take refugees. There was not that certainty in other camps, except Hongkong. Thus the thrust of the resettlement efforts continued to be elsewhere.

In all the camps there were differences in administration and in some facets of the lives of the refugees themselves. But there were also similarities —the sense of displacement was strong and unmistakable. Often there was lassitude. Often there was boredom and lack of hope. Families were broken and sometimes never reunited, and in spite of their daily activities and functions, many, many refugees had an aura of sorrow and tragedy about them that was understandable, given their circumstances. There were severe cases of melancholia, signs of brain damage and bone deformities in the children, and once the initial hungers had been satisfied, some refugees began to demonstrate all the symptoms of people who had been traumatized by terror and hunger. What will become of these refugees? How will they adjust to new lives in new countries, and will they ever be able to make strong contributions to their new societies? The questions are easy, the answers, at this early stage, impossible.

settling permanently among the ice blue fjords of Norway. They do not seem to mind.

Ly Dang Khoa began their story:

> There were forty-seven of us, fourteen men, sixteen women, and seventeen children. We did not pay to get out, as many have had to do; we simply escaped. We used a boat that the Vietnamese security people were used to seeing go up and down the river at Can Tho, and we took it one night and went down the river and out into the open sea. Soon we were too far out for anyone to see us . . .

As he tells of the escape, others from his group begin to gather and stand close, nodding and reliving their adventure. They have the look of people who have seen the successful end of a dangerous gamble, but the young children push up against the adults' legs, seeking security in the touch.

> . . . so it was a small boat but not as crowded as some other boats have been. We were eight days at sea, heading in the general direction of Singapore. We saw five ships, and perhaps they saw us or perhaps not. Then two of our children died. They had been ill, but not for long, and suddenly they were dead. We slipped them over the side of the boat into the sea.
>
> A few days later we were picked up by a Norwegian ship, the *Stolt Sheaf,* and soon after that we were in Singapore. Some of us now will go to Norway.

Had they been captured it would have meant long prison sentences, but Ly Dang Khoa said it was preferable to take the risk than to look forward to years of economic hardships.

> There is only two kilos of rice per person per month. The black market is flourishing in Vietnam. There are not many things for sale. New supplies that we see in Vietnam all go to government officials.

At the Hawkins Road camp there is plenty of food and plenty of hope. The refugees here are a people who cheated death, and they turn to life with a renewed vigor. The camp is clean by Asian rural standards. The people are well-dressed, and from the large, rambling houses containing the refugees you can hear laughter as the women prepare the traditional savory Vietnamese dishes.

Before driving out to the Hawkins Road camp, we had been told by Paul Wedel, South Asia Manager for United Press International, that the camp was better organized than those of most governments. He may be right. There is a reception center, a chapel, a post office. There is a camp organization which begins with the camp leader and works through all the facets of needs the refugees now have. The camp has a young man who appears to be of college age and turns out to be a hardworking doctor who has organized and maintained a pharmacy and consultation room. There is a single telephone, in constant use. In the dusty streets the young boys were playing with marbles, the girls skipping rope, in the manner of children everywhere. There was much bantering from house to house, and on one porch of a house a man was swinging gently in a makeshift hammock and reading a newspaper. Incredibly, the entire camp projected an air of normality, and yet none of these people would be situated here more than ninety days (although the figure slips a bit in special cases; the Singapore government is not too rigid, secure in the knowledge that one way or another, all the refugees will eventually be gone from Singapore).

Strolling through the camp we were surprised to hear someone saying "Good morning, how are you?" in perfect Norwegian. A handsome Norwegian lady was teaching the rudiments of the language to the new arrivals, and in other parts of the camp, two other Norwegian teachers were carrying out the same task. (When we tried to photograph one at her chalkboard, she blushed and erased the board. She had been teaching both language and simple math, and suddenly noticed she had gotten her additions wrong.)

The camp is financed by the United Nations, which pays the Singapore government rent of some 300 Singapore dollars per month (about $150) on each of the housing units. The funds are plentiful enough in Singapore to allow each refugee an allowance of $2.50 in Singapore dollars, sufficient for occasional snacks and a movie in the city. In spite of the edict allowing no more than one thousand refugees at a time in Singapore, the government tolerates the roughly fifteen hundred here because these refugees are definitely moving on. As they wander about the island, the refugees blend in nicely, and there have been no major incidents between them and the island's residents.

In the reception center of the Hawkins Road camp is a sign which says, "Today families are forced to flee their homes because of their beliefs. If they survive, they are refugees." A second sign reads, "Your sympathy cannot help a refugee. But it is a beginning." Underneath the two signs we found a pleasant young woman, a U.N. employee who would not be quoted by name but said, without much preamble, that the Hawkins Road camp was serving a psychological purpose as well as meeting physical needs.

What you see here is a collection of people who have been taught class divisions by the French and war by the Americans —and by that I simply mean that a military or governing presence is their only perception of Westerners. The best thing we do here goes beyond taking care of their food, clothing, and shelter. It's letting them touch us, hug us, see us unhappy, see us in real situations, letting the children sit in our laps. They are beginning to regard us as real people, as normal people, not so different.

Before she has finished talking a little girl wanders into the room and unerringly, as if drawn by a magnet, she scampers to the young woman and climbs unhesitatingly and without asking into her lap. All over the camp it is the same; the small children are desperate for affection and they run, with a look of hope and longing in their large, liquid eyes, to almost any adult.

Despite the temporary nature of the camp, despite the knowledge that the Hawkins Road camp itself would be moved a few miles away in the near future, the refugees give the camp an air of stability because they have so urgently tried to turn it into a home where the young people can feel secure. Part of the stable atmosphere comes from the U.N. workers like the young woman with the child in her lap. Much of it comes from the refugees' remembrance of the lives they lived in Vietnam, and the wild gamble they took by climbing into the crowded and creaking boats. The sense of hope and purpose they project reaches out and envelops visitors and is refreshing, if a little surprising. It prompted a visiting U.S. senator to tell U.N. workers that the refugees reminded him of Americans of an earlier time who still believed in the American dream—that if they got an education, worked hard and lived decent lives, they could not fail to become successes.

"It's true," says the young U.N. worker. "They are hopeful and confident. You see, this is an unusual camp, probably the most fortunate one the refugees could have reached. They know they will be accepted somewhere, and after what they've been through they're anxious to get settled and start a new life. If you want to become encouraged about man's basic decency in the face of all the odds, this is the place to do it."

The situation puts one's values into sharp focus. By many Western standards the camp is almost squalid, but there is a taste, a smell, a sense of rebirth that is as firm and tangible as the grass and trees. They are a campful of transients but crime is not a problem; they will go their separate ways, but for this time and place they adhere to camp rules and principles; they face new languages, new job situations, perhaps even new prejudices and certainly unforeseen difficulties, but there is laughter in the camp and even some budding love affairs. The senator was right. These displaced people project a frontier spirit and a boisterous sense of adventure.

But at least one refugee in the camp is haunted by memories. It is his second escape from the same oppressors, twenty-six years apart, and this time he left behind a wife with little hope of seeing her again. He is unable to stop thinking about her sacrifice, and his acceptance of it. And when he finally reached freedom with his four children, the Americans, with whom he had worked for years in Saigon, refused to grant them permission to enter the United States. At the age of fifty, with four children and a language barrier, he is facing the prospects of living in Japan on whatever employment he can find—and without his wife.

This is the story Nguyen (not his real name) told while sitting on a small knoll overlooking the Hawkins Road camp. Nguyen looks at least ten years older than he is—unusual for Asians—and there is gray in his slight goatee. He has cheekbones even more prominent than most Vietnamese, and his wiry body could be that of a schoolboy. What is remarkable about him is not only his excellent English but also his expressive eyes which flash anger or reflect sorrow as the memories flood him:

First you must understand why we left. It was not just the economic conditions, bad as they are. It was because we had no freedom of speech and we had to lie all the time. We had not much freedom of anything, but mostly I got tired of having to lie. If we were asked by the government if we had enough food we had to say yes, even though we had little food. If we said no, there was not enough to eat, there would be some form of punishment. Especially, and this was very important to them, if some foreigner happened to ask you if you had enough food you must say yes, even if you are starving. If they offer you food, you must say no, you are not hungry.

I have heard there are four thousand Russians in Vietnam. I have not seen that many, but there are some in Ho Chi Minh City. You can see them around the port areas, even though we Vietnamese are not allowed near the ports. They live well, while many of our people are living out in the forests without enough food or water.

It was going near the port in Ho Chi Minh City that got me caught by the security forces. To go anywhere in Vietnam today, you need travel permits, and I went near the port to see what boats were going in and out. I was caught without papers and detained for three hours before they let me go. I told them I was looking for my mother-in-law, who lived in the area. If they checked they would find she really did live in the area. Later, I was caught again and told the same story and got away without punishment. Lucky. And all the time I was thinking of escape.

It was the second time in my life I was planning to escape. In 1954, after the talks in Geneva, I felt I had to leave my village. We lived near Haiphong, in the North. Many people were leaving. I was a Catholic and a young man, and I felt it would be better for me if I went south. My parents were dead, but they had owned a gold shop in Haiphong, so my sister and I went down to the docks where ships were taking people aboard. We just walked on, onto a ship called the *Marine Serpent.* We brought out two hundred gold bars with us and settled in Saigon. My sister still lives near there, in Bien Hoa.

I was a typical young man. I bought a car, got into an accident, spent a lot of money. I enlisted in the French army and spent the next two years in Saigon as a private first class—teaching men how to drive! Later on I worked as a civilian for French construction companies, and then for at least ten years I worked for American construction firms in Vietnam. I also owned a small photography shop in Saigon.

When the end came for the Americans in Vietnam, I knew it was the beginning of trouble for us. I had married and had children, and my wife and I discussed many times how we would get out of Vietnam, especially to give the children freedom and the opportunity for a better life than they would have in Vietnam today. After the Americans had been gone a little while, we decided we would go too. The government hated us northerners who had gone south because we had wanted to. They wanted to kill us off and regarded us as risky people. A lot of people were put into relocation camps where the government said life was heavenly. But it really was terrible. Whole families were lured into the camps by a simple method. The men were taken by force and their families told if they wanted to see them again they had to join them in the camps.

My wife and I stayed out of the camps and planned for five years how we would escape. We knew it had to be by boat, but the police were very careful not to let us near the water. Finally, a friend who had a boat said he he would take us out, that he was taking out a lot of people. We prepared to leave, but each day made escape more difficult. When we finally got ready to go, my wife made a great sacrifice.

We knew that the security forces had set up a system of reporting in each neighborhood, almost on each street. If a house looked deserted, as if no one lived there anymore, someone—no one knew who it was—would report it to the police and they would check immediately. So my wife told me to take the children and leave. She would stay behind and fool the police into thinking we were all at home. Another reason was that if we failed to escape we might be able to get home again without anyone finding out we had tried. It was a terrible thing, but I left her standing there in the doorway of the house. I took the children—three girls ages sixteen, eleven, and four, and my seven-year-old son—and we joined the others on the boat.

At first I thought we had made a bad mistake. The boat was thirty-six feet long and six feet wide, and there were 174 people on board. When I got on I had to sit with my knees drawn up so there would be room for others, and I sat that way for most of three days, only occasionally getting up to stretch. We sailed at night out of My Tho, near Ho Chi Minh City, carrying hardly any food or water because we wanted to make as much room as possible. We even threw some of the food overboard to make room. In two days we were drinking the water used to cool the boat's engine.

Out on the open ocean we passed close to a Panamanian ship, but it refused to stop for us. A day later we saw a Russian ship coming close, and we sailed to meet it. As we got closer together the Russian captain gestured for us to stand off, not to come any closer. The ship would not pick us up, and the captain said he would shoot if we came closer. Before the ship sailed away someone threw us three cans of water, about twenty liters in each can. The water tasted like machine water of some kind, but we drank it. The next day a Japanese ship called the *Canadian Highway* stopped and picked us up. Our boat was truly lucky.

But I did not feel lucky—my wife was still in Ho Chi Minh City. I felt that if I could get to America I might be able to get her out. I thought the Americans would take me because I had worked for them so long, because I speak good English, and especially because I had the four children, and Americans like children.

But they told me the United States could take only so many refugees, and that because I had no blood relative in America I would have to go somewhere else. It now seems I will go to Japan with the children because it was a Japanese ship that picked us up.

I don't want to go to Japan. The language is very difficult for me, and I am just too old to try very hard to learn it. I don't know what I will do in Japan. Somehow it seems to me that I will have more trouble getting my wife out if I am in Japan instead of America. I think constantly about getting her out. I think about how she stayed behind so we could escape. I think life is very difficult, isn't it?''

VII

The Uncertain Future

To leave home, friends, and country and become a refugee is an act of desperation. In Indochina, to throw yourself on the mercy of your neighboring countries is to take a calculated risk. Survival is at stake; to be impelled to sail or trek away from what was once a friendly environment, now become a nightmare, is to exercise an option only once removed from death by starvation or torture or as part of a deliberate genocide, as in Cambodia.

The refugees along the Thai-Cambodian border are, in desperate circumstances, and no one knows better than they that their camps are temporary, and the future is uncertain and probably dangerous. While they gratefully accept the relief measures being provided, there is a basic mistrust of such efforts, a sense that somewhere, somehow, they are going to have to make their own way. This feeling is fed by the nationalistic elements among the Khmer Serei and Khmer Rouge, who believe that they can drive the Vietnamese out of Cambodia and retake the country. This is why many of them regard the camps along the border as sanctuaries, giving them breathing space and time so they can slip into guerrilla strongholds in Cambodia and resume the battle against the forces of the Vietnamese puppet, Heng Samrin.

This sense of purpose is not lost on the Thai government, which worries about it because it fears the Vietnamese may spill over the border in hot pursuit or in a deliberate offensive, and carry the long running Indochina struggle finally into peaceful Thailand. Such a move would also put enormous pressures on the United States, which would have to make the decision to support or not support the Thai military if such an event takes place.

At this writing there are conflicting reports of the Vietnamese intentions; if the offensive does not come this year, will it follow in the next? The best military estimate is that it would take place in a dry season, sometime between November and March. This would allow the Heng Samrin/Vietnamese forces to employ their tanks with some effectiveness. The border area around Aranyaprathet, where the larger camps are located, is ideal country for tank warfare. There have been reports of increased reconnaissance and intelligence gathering by the Vietnamese, and the Vietnamese have scarcely paused in their steady denunciation of Thailand for providing sanctuaries. A concerned U.S. State Department has called on both the Vietnamese government and the Soviet Union, whose support of the Vietnamese is no secret, "to refrain from any action which would threaten Thailand's security and integrity or endanger the well-being and safety of the noncombatants in the refugee concentrations along the border." The proportion of guerrillas to noncombatants in the border areas is anyone's guess. There are at least 50,000 Vietnamese just across the Cambodian border, however, and they are a battle-hardened army. Opposite them are the 500,000 or so refugees in the border camps, and another 150,000 in holding camps in the interior of Thailand. No one is sure that of the great number of refugees, anything like 50,000 of them are guerrillas, and even if there are that many, they are not as well equipped or as experienced as the Vietnamese. Not unless Thailand's military forces, with outside aid, opposed the Vietnamese offensive, would there be any sustained or successful blocking force on the border. The innocent bystanders, of course, are the refugees, who already have plenty of problems in the camps—a shortage of water, a lack of privacy, food supplies sometimes intercepted by camp committees which want to sell them instead of distributing them free, uncertainty about resettlement in a foreign country, a lack of quick processing which often keeps them in camps for years, broken families and fear for loved ones whose whereabouts are unknown, the just-surfacing realization that many of the children have mental disorders and probably permanent bone damage as a result of malnutrition, increasing cases of infidelity, and sometimes a general amoral behavior and attitude born of hopelessness.

As the tragedy of the refugees continued, as aid programs developed, as some nations responded and others held back, a number of technical questions developed. The questions were concerned with methodology, logistics, extent of aid, air cargo capabilities, truck routes, and diplomatic moves within the United Nations. Implied in many, if not all, of these situations was the belief that the refugees were deserving of help, and the world should provide assistance. Despite all the efforts, perhaps even because of them, the basic question kept reappearing: what does the world owe the refugees? Am I my brother's keeper?

To raise the question of morality is to place yet another overlay on top of the facade of Indochina, a region notorious for its penchant for doing violence to itself. For like the religions of the area, morality has a different definition from country to country. In Thailand, the government took the position initially that it believed the state's first duty was the protection of its country and its citizens; a position that seems to be supported in deed if not in word throughout the rest of the world. It is one reason the Thais hesitated when confronted with the thousands of fleeing refugees streaming across its border. Similarly, the Malaysians voiced their opinion that Vietnam was upsetting the normal balance of power in Southeast Asia by dumping its unwanted citizens on other nations—a deliberate effort to undermine the political and economic status quo. It was a view that the refugees may or may not have even considered; they only knew they were cast adrift in a highly volatile and dangerous situation. What they were hearing were threats from Malaysia that they would be shot if they tried to land. The Malaysian position was amplified by statements which claimed that it was a matter of national security when hordes of people from another country were expelled from that country and attempted to move in on a nearby state. Despite the pathetic condition of the refugees, they were regarded as something akin to an invasion force. In Singapore, in Hongkong, in Indonesia, they were taken in, but not with enthusiasm. Instead of being greeted as escapees from a totalitarian regime, from cruel and inhumane conditions; they were looked upon as pawns in a cynical move by Vietnam to make money by exporting people for gold; they were seen as guerrillas seeking sanctuary before returning to the combat in Cambodia, hence risking Thailand's neutrality; they were regarded as a Vietnamese fifth column which might be loyal to Vietnam in the event of a wider war in Southeast Asia; they were seen as a nuisance which had to be dealt with. Few, if any, refugees were received with open arms and congratulations on their successful escape from tyranny.

Inside Cambodia, where for four long years the Pol Pot regime had systematically and brutally murdered the intellectuals, doctors, lawyers, schoolteachers, and even anyone who wore eyeglasses, widespread famine took many of the lives that Pol Pot's henchmen missed. Vietnam's Christmas Day invasion of 1978 was timed to coincide with the period of primary rice harvest. Both the Vietnamese and the opposing Khmer Rouge forces used crop destruction and denial tactics, bringing on the loss of approximately 90 percent of the rice crop, the staple of the Cambodian diet. The Cambodian forces fought each other—Khmer Rouge against the Vietnamese-backed People's Republic of Kampuchea—while the Khmer Serei fought almost everyone. There were, as a result, massive population shifts, for the most part away from agricultural lands, disrupting the normal May–June plantings. Thus the yield from the August 1979 harvest was 10 percent of normal, that of the December 1979 primary harvest about 8 percent.

If in the long Asian perspective the situation today is not much different from the situation over the past hundreds of years, it does not justify the unrelenting cruelty. Just as man has accepted the evolution of technology, so should he be aware of the evolution of human rights and attempt to ameliorate atrocities committed upon his fellowman. And there is no justification in the West for any holier-than-thou attitude, for the West's record is no better.

Another facet of the morality question turned up in the United Nations. On 5 November 1979, the United Nations hosted a worldwide conference in which fifty-one nations pledged their contributions to efforts to keep the Cambodian people from extinction. The Soviet Union did not contribute, claiming it had delivered, up to that time, some $85 million in food and other supplies to Cambodia. That claim took on cynical overtones when it was pointed out that a large part of the Russian contribution was for the feeding of the Vietnamese troops occupying Cambodia. Such actions evoke all the old claims that Indochina is merely the locale of a surrogate war among the superpowers; the United States, the Soviet Union, and the People's Republic of China.

The authors of this book are well aware that by the time it is in print, a Russian-sanctioned Vietnamese offensive could have taken place. Many reporters and other observers along the border have predicted it, in spite of assurances from Vietnam's Deputy Foreign Minister Phan Hien that no such action was planned by Hanoi. At this writing the threat of a Vietnamese invasion remains a large concern in Indochina.

One thing that makes the future uncertain for the refugees is the highly politicized nature of the problem. No sooner had the Heng Samrin forces taken control of Cambodia than the United States initiated its stand-off attitude, a move to punish Hanoi. Within months, most of America's allies had suspended or cut back their assistance programs to Hanoi. The United States was also uncertain about any kind of aid to Cambodia and, in fact, was either uncertain there actually was a famine or unwilling to admit it. The reason: aid of any kind to Cambodia would strengthen the Heng Samrin forces, i.e., the Vietnamese forces, and continue the subjugation of the Cambodian people. In an article in the 18 November 1979 edition of *The Washington Post,* reporter Elizabeth Becker quoted a Washington source: "It was easier for policy reasons to wait to see if the 'worst case' scenario was accurate. In July the CIA and some members of the State Department were still talking about the famine as if it were a propaganda tool of Hanoi to get the United States to feed and recognize the Heng Samrin government." All of this meant little or nothing to people who were starving to death, but such global concerns in the future could once again have a negative effect on the rehabilitation and resettlement of refugees—in Indochina or elsewhere.

Tragically, the refugees in the border camps, unlike the majority of the boat people, have few choices. The boat people at least could look forward to resettlement somewhere at some point; they had, and have, a tangible future although it may be in a strange land with a whole new set of problems. The border refugees, on the other hand, have few appealing choices. Their options now are resettlement elsewhere, integration into Thai society, return to Cambodia, permanent residence in the camps, or some unforeseen choice such as permanent homes on some Indonesian island where they can keep their families and, hopefully, their culture intact. This last option, by far the most desirable, had not been made available up to early 1980.

Resettlement, the option preferred by some refugees, looks to be a slow process, leading to a prolonged stay in the border camps. Refugees are not moved as quickly as the boat people because they lack the overseas relatives, the connections, the skills, and the ambitions—and in many cases the funds—of the predominantly Chinese boat people. Additionally, the processing machinery of the border is not as efficient as in the camps of the boat people, partly for the humanitarian reasons mentioned earlier: the boat people are accepted and moved on because if they are not resettled promptly, the first-asylum countries will stop accepting them, dooming thousands to death at sea or a sad return to Vietnam and whatever fate would await them there. Once again, forces beyond their control play a large role in the lives of the border refugees.

For the refugees to attempt to integrate into Thai society is not a satisfactory answer. The Thais probably would not accept them with grace given the ancient hatreds and the current mistrust. The refugees found sanctuary in Thailand primarily because of the intervention of the United States—and credit must be given to the great personal efforts of U.S. Ambassador to Thailand Morton Abramowitz—after an initial hostility by the Thais which saw some forty thousand refugees driven back across the border at gunpoint.

Settlement in enclaves along the inhospitable border is also not an answer, for there is inadequate land, water, agriculture, industry, and other necessities for self-sufficiency. To establish these rural ghettoes would be to create a new set of difficulties for the Thais and for the refugees themselves, and would entail a massive and continuing relief program which the world might not be prepared to undertake.

Even more uncertain is the issue of voluntary repatriation. Such a move would by necessity require from the Vietnamese invaders of Cambodia the assurance of fair treatment—an assurance which, in turn, would demand some enforcement by the rest of the world. The accomplishment of this demands resolutions of staggering problems, involving political, social, and military considerations. The reality is that it probably could not be accomplished at all. This would leave the refugees in a situation every bit as precarious as the one they now face.

Perhaps the only workable solution is resettlement, slow and cumbersome as it may be. Barring the happy eventuality of mass resettlement on neutral ground, such as an island or other landmass suitable for them, the best hope for the refugees now appears to be in other countries, far from the gentle land they once knew. Such resettlement has its own intrinsic problems; the Cambodians, by and large, are an agrarian people unused to the pace and complexities of a developed, industrialized country. Most of them are unskilled in Western terms, although few people can get more production out of a plot of land. They are unused to extreme climatic changes. They would have difficulty competing in the West in terms of employment in middle to upper-level positions.

Coupled with this is the understandable reluctance by many to leave their homeland. The refugees from Laos especially, as well as the Cambodians, seem to have little desire to relocate. They entertain hopes of seeing their countries wrenched back from the Communist overlords, and they give little thought to going elsewhere. But part of the tragedy of the refugees is that they may have little or nothing to say about their own future.

Westerners may be unaccustomed to thinking of Asians in terms of nationalism or patriotism, but these are factors in Indochinese lives. Each country of that embattled peninsula has its own version of history, enjoys its own folklore, contemplates its own future. While it is true that some of them are more nationalistic than others, all share a sense of nationhood to some degree. In parts of Indochina, particularly among the hill tribes in Laos and Vietnam, there is a loyalty first to family, second to village, third to tribe. Often there is no fourth. Still, a semblance of nationalism is present and seems to grow stronger in the face of such oppression as the Vietnamese invasion of Cambodia. Added to old antagonisms, it is impetus for conflict. This nationalism adds yet another factor to the question so prevalent in early 1980, and for which there is no immediate and permanent answer—what is to happen to the refugees?

Meanwhile, efforts continue to make their primitive situation as bearable as possible under the circumstances.

So far, these efforts have been made in the spirit of sympathy and humanitarianism. A major portion of the aid, in the form of funds, medicines, and manpower, has come from countries which have taken in a relatively small portion of the refugees themselves. For, except in Israel, for whom the ingathering of exiles is their raison d'etre as well as their raison d'etat, large waves of refugees are rarely met with open arms. It now appears that the refugee problem will be a long-range situation. If this is the case, and if the situation worsens, there is always the possibility that the inclination to continue aid will erode.

While the UNHCR will presumably continue its good work, its operations must depend on the contributions from individual U.N. member nations. At present politics do not interfere with humanitarianism. But if the geopolitical situation continues to worsen, these two factors may well come into open conflict. At that point, the parliaments of the member countries which feel that these forces are in conflict will be reluctant to vote funds for refugee aid.

At the receiving end of the refugee process, residents of at least two camps in Thailand told representatives of the U.S. government investigating reports of irregularities, of how they were required to pay for services. The camps were at Nong Khai and Ubon in Thailand, and had been established as early as 1975. In these camps, the Laotian refugees said they had to pay Thai officials or other Laotian refugees first for admission to the camp, later for such basics as food, water, shelter, and medical care. To operate small businesses inside the camps, they also had to pay Thai officials. The refugees further claimed that Thai officials were diverting food supplies destined for the camps, and that refugees also had to pay the officials to receive mail from relatives overseas. And to note the acts of piracy against the boat people, the rapes and robberies and murders, is to chronicle man in his basest moments. There is a bitter irony in the terrible reports that according to estimates, thousands of the Cambodian children under the age of six have died in agony and despair during the International Year of the Child.

It is one of the failures of our time that we have gone from gunpower to hydrogen bombs without a simultaneous advance in our moral outlooks. The constitutions of nearly every government, including those of the Soviet Union and all its satellites, contain pious phrases affirming protection of the rights of their citizens. But the predicament of the refugees demonstrates that the natural rights of man are, as Edmund Burke put it, mere abstractions, no more than "entailed inheritances." Burke's attack on the French Declaration of the Rights of Man, which he called a "digest of anarchy," focused attention on the fragility of the "rights" theory—the "inalienable" rights of individual liberty and property are inalienable only if all nations define them and uphold them. Thomas Paine was concerned with the individual's protection from the state; if the individual's rights were protected *from* the state, only then could those rights be effectively protected *by* the state.

The Nazi holocaust and the misery of the refugees who escaped the ovens brought about a widespread insistence that human rights be internationally defined, recognized, and protected. At the United Nations conference in 1945 in San Francisco, many delegations urged the inclusion in the U.N. Charter of an unequivocal declaration of human rights. But the conference decided that such a proposal required careful drafting, and it was not until 1948 that the Universal Declaration of Human Rights was adopted by the U.N. General Assembly. The declaration received a unanimous vote (Saudi Arabia, which permitted slavery, South Africa, and the six Soviet block countries abstained).

The declaration provided specific definitions of the rights of: life, liberty, and the security of person; freedom from arbitrary arrest, detention, or exile; freedom of thought, conscience, and religion; and freedom of peaceful assembly and association. Unfortunately it was unspecific about enforcement.

Eleanor Roosevelt, one of the principal authors, pointed out that the declaration was not "an international agreement. It is not and does not purport to be a statement of law or of legal obligation."

Since the adoption of the declaration we have only to review the history of intolerance and the resultant millions of refugees to see that statements of human rights, natural rights, inalienable rights, however defined, are little more than expressions of hopeless idealism, hypocrisy, or shaky morality.

The morality of the refugee problem itself is tangled. On the one hand the problems—and their moral solutions—are simple and direct. Human beings are deprived of their rights in their own land, take them in and give them their rights in your land. Human beings are homeless, give them shelter. Human beings are hungry, feed them. Human beings are dying, save them. On the other hand, the problems are subtle and the solutions difficult. Is our first moral obligation to our own security (ask the inhabitants of the first-asylum states)? Will the refugees continue to flood the border camps and towns, eventually moving deeper inland to occupy scarce lands and consume scarce food? Will the refugees become permanent, unwanted residents? Will our acceptance of the refugees encourage oppressive regimes to expel their political undesirables? Will hostile states attempt to destabilize their neighbor nations by flooding them with refugees?

Will our long-standing tradition of political asylum stimulate intolerant governments to evict their citizens who ask only that their human rights be acknowledged and respected?

Does aid to refugees, in effect, generate new waves of refugees?

The questions multiply and come as swiftly as the monsoon rains. In the abstract they are the stuff of college themes and debating society positions. In the realities of Indochinese relationships they are of vital import. In the squalor of a refugee encampment where people live still fearful of the future, there are no such questions. There is only living or dying.

Politics have not, as a rule, played a part in the work of the voluntary agencies. But the national agencies, who depend for funds on the contributions of individual citizens, may well see their revenue drop if those citizens, like their governments, feel that the political considerations in helping refugees are greater than the humanitarian aspects. It is not for financial reasons that the Soviet Union, a member of the United Nations, has not contributed one kopeck to aid Eastern European refugees.

Early in 1980, the authors wrote to Poul Hartling, the United Nations High Commissioner for Refugees. We asked him for a statement on international responsibility for refugee assistance. Hartling replied as follows:

The dimensions of the refugee problem across the world have dramatically increased over the last few years but the essential problem of refugees, and the necessary solutions to those problems, have been the same throughout history and across the world. Refugees need to be fed, clothed and sheltered; they need to find new homes if they cannot return to their old ones, and be assisted to attain self-sufficiency in them. They want to go back home if they can, and more often than not need help to do so. Fundamental needs in the face of the experience of exile are the same for everyone in the human family, across the world. In our present-day world of unrest and conflict, these humanitarian principles should be consistently recognized and respected.

The responsibility for refugees is a universal one. The world's more privileged nations have learned that they cannot share selectively in the responsibility, by offering only money or medicine. Various countries of first asylum have had to put up with an intolerable strain on their resources, which in many cases are quite slender, in order to shelter and sustain refugees by themselves.

When the countries of a region provide temporary asylum and camp facilities, other nations must offer resettlement prospects and the prospect of new lives for the refugees—each country providing what it can and what its resources will permit in order to alleviate the common burden.

The support of the international community for refugee work is an affirmation and acknowledgment of mankind's responsibility for the dispossessed. In this book the authors pose the question, ''Am I my brother's keeper?'' The answer is yes, and many countries have backed up their answer with tangible support. Such support is not confined merely to the wealthier nations who constitute our traditional donors. While 90 percent of the financial assistance to UNHCR comes from a dozen countries, most of the world's refugees would not survive without the generosity of several developing countries, which shelter these unfortunate exiles despite the limited nature of the countries' own national resources. Thus, in Africa, the local governments often contribute large tracts of land, provide administrative personnel, and meet as much of the refugees' needs as they possibly can. At the same time, the nations which have done so much to provide UNHCR with resources to cope with refugee needs also contribute to our endeavors by offering resettlement places to refugees.

Resettlement is, unfortunately, indispensable to the achievement of solutions to refugee problems when, for example, refugees seek asylum in countries where they are not welcome or into which they cannot easily integrate. It is, of course, encouraging that nations which are often thousands of kilometers removed from refugee situations open their doors in welcome to the uprooted. This demonstrates once again that, though refugee problems may never cease to exist, the world will continue to be aware of the refugees' needs and increasingly willing, on an international basis, to help them.

It is gratifying to those of us in refugee work that this is indeed happening, though of course much more can be done. The programs to benefit refugees across the world are the products of an extraordinary partnership between international bodies such as UNHCR, governments, and ordinary people—whether organized as voluntary agencies or simply as individuals who support their government's efforts on behalf of refugees. UNHCR does not operate in a vacuum; indeed, it could not. In its crucial task of protecting, settling, and assisting refugees, UNHCR benefits from the help and support of agencies and institutions across the world.

Universality is therefore central to UNHCR's work. The Office has the delicate responsibility of safeguarding the rights and interests of refugees while at the same time retaining the indispensable support of governments. The guiding principle of UNHCR, enshrined in the statute of its office, is that it is nonpolitical and humanitarian. UNHCR has to deal with countries which, while sheltering refugees and supporting the work of the Office, may also be the countries of origin of significant refugee groups. It has to cope with the problems of countries of first asylum, where large refugee populations are not always welcome. Nonetheless, the widespread and unquestionable support for UNHCR's work is constantly reaffirmed in General Assembly resolutions and in practice across the globe.

Regardless of the source and amount of funds and other assistance, and regardless of the UNHCR's unceasing efforts, the refugees cannot be compensated for what they have lost, nor be assured of a future. They have suffered incredible hardships, from which some will never recover. The mental damages, the psychological problems, the sense of rootlessness—these will not disappear in the near future, if ever. It is tragic speculation to think of the disrupted lives, the lost homes and farms, the death that came sometimes swiftly, sometimes with horrifying slowness. There have been some successes and some small, gratifying steps to save lives and keep families intact. But the dark side of the story is that the problem has not ended, and indeed, may not have an end.

*A modern Pie(
Piper, this teacher i
mobbed by children i
the Khao I Dan,
Camp along the Tha(
Cambodian border. H
walks through cam,
shouting words
numbers, in English
The children echo him*

Scott C.S. Stone

Scott C.S. Stone

New refugees being helped to off-load at Khao I Dang.

New refugees enter the Khao I Dang Camp. Thai soldiers man the gates and checkpoints.

Scott C.S. Stone

A temporary camp near
Camp 007, next to
the Thai village of Ban
Nong Samet. Refugees
were sent here due to
"chaotic" conditions in
the camp, so termed
by the Thai military.

A pensive child in
a refugee camp
at Ban Nong
Samet on the Thai-
Cambodian border.

An infant sits forlornly in a section of a refugee camp at Sakaew, Thailand, his past a traumatic impression, his future uncertain.

Inside a temporary camp for refugees near Ban Nong Samet, along the Thai-Cambodian border. Despite the fact that most refugees were well dressed, conditions were primitive

Scott C.S. Stone

Scott C.S. Stone

Scott C.S. Stone

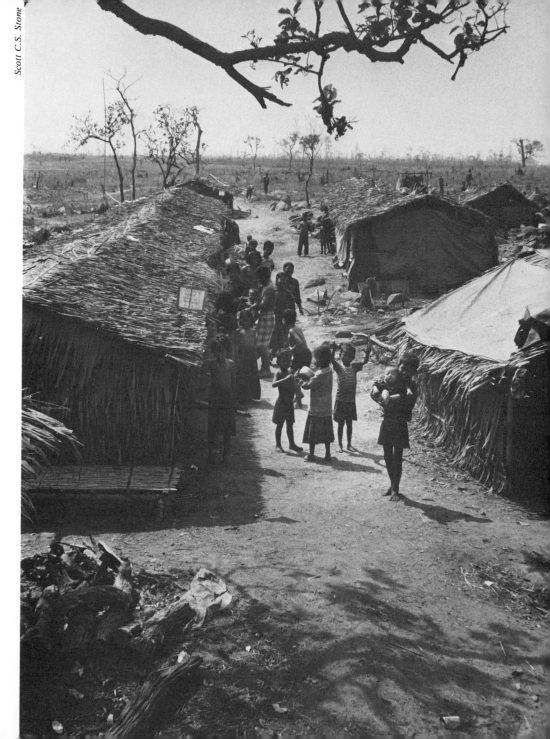

Lacking proper warehousing, bags of rice are off-loaded and stored outdoors at Khao I Dang.

Scott C.S. Stone

Street scene in the camp on the Thai-Cambodian border; a waterless, somewhat desolate sector.

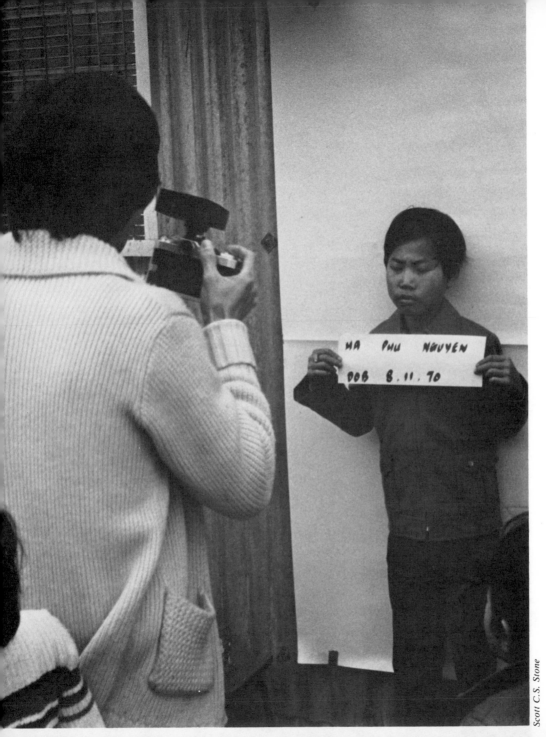

A young ethnic Chinese from Vietnam is photographed for his passport; it will take him from the Sham Shui Po refugee camp in Hongkong to a new life in a permanent home.

A Thai trooper in a uncommon show friendliness to refuge boys near Ban Nor Samet. Most Tha seemed reserved wi the Khmer refugee

Scott C.S. Stone

Scott C.S. Stone

Scott C.S. Stone

The headquarters area of Camp 204 near the Thai village of Ban Non Mak Mun, one of the more "unsettled" refugee camps which has been the scene of skirmishes between Khmer factions. The camp is extensive, reaching into Cambodia.

The barbershop in Kai Tak East refugee camp. There were few amenities, but the usual amount of barbershop chatter.

A Chinese refugee child, her face marred by sores but her future brighter than most refugees, waits in the Kai Tak East refugee camp in Hongkong for resettlement.

Scott C.S. Stone

Inside the refuge camp at Ban Non Ma Mun. The Khme factions gave the cam an air of menace, an most refugees here wer wary and cautious

Scott C.S. Stone

Scott C.S. Stone

Hospital ward in the camp at Sakaew. By modern medical standards, conditions are somewhat primitive, but by Asian standards are superior to facilities and personnel throughout much of Indochina.

Senators S. I. Hayakawa and Carl Levin, trailed by aides, tour the refugee camp at Sakaew, Thailand.

Wood carriers in Sakaew led by a small child doing his bit.

In the Sakaew refugee camp, Thailand water is hauled by the oldest method.

Scott C.S. Stone

*A young girl plays
beneath the ever-present
laundry at Hongkong's
Sham Shui Po Camp.*

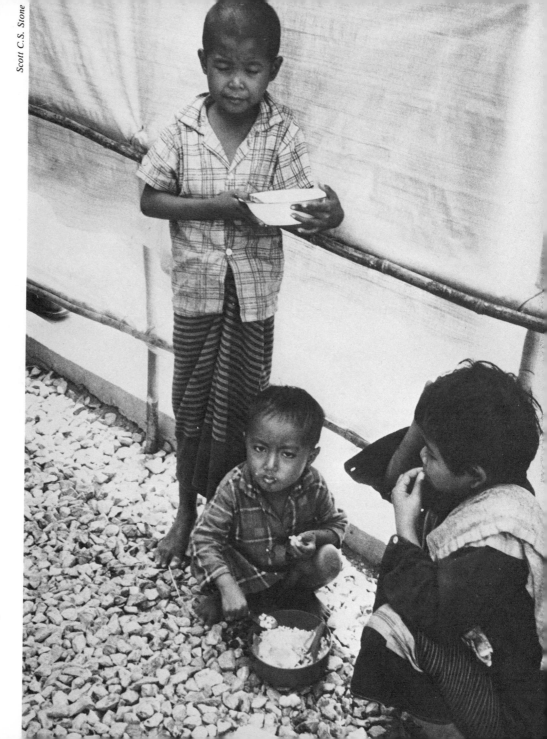

Scott C.S. Stone

*Children feed
themselves in
the Intensive Feeding
Section of the camp
at Sakaew.*

Scott C.S. Stone

Children wait outside a processing office at a refugee camp in Hongkong.
Assured of resettlement, they will be in new homes within a few months.
Meanwhile, refugees add 50,000 bodies to overcrowded Hongkong.

PART II

VIII

A Review of Refugees around the World—1917-1944

Fifty-seven years before the Vietnamese took to the boats, another group of refugees, on the other side of the world, were leaving their homes. These were the refugees who fled in the wake of the Russian Revolution of 1917 and 1918. The mindless persecution by Lenin's security services, the Cheka, and the ineffective counterrevolutionary struggles of the White Russians forced more than one and a half million Russians to flee their country. The majority of these exiles, expecting that the Communist regime would collapse of its own ineptitude and that they would soon return home, went to nearly every country contiguous to Russia, and also to France, to the United States, and to Japan.

Unlike the measures taken to resettle the boat people, assistance to the Russian refugees was grounded on the conviction that the new Soviet regime had a short life expectancy. Thus funds provided by governments and private relief agencies in countries of refuge were considered short-term emergency expenditures. Nowhere was there any thought of permanently resettling the refugees. Nor was there any consideration given to temporarily moving the Russian refugees to areas where they might find better social and economic circumstances. Those plays and novels of the 1930's in which waiters, fencing masters, and dance instructors were Russian grand dukes, Cossack colonels, or just ordinary aristocrats, had a basis in fact.

As the years wore on and the Soviet government refused to collapse, the nations harboring these unfortunate, homesick Russian refugees came to the realization that the problem was not going to be solved through early repatriation. In 1920 and 1921 many of the host governments then sought to dump their wards on, and into, other countries. In the post-World War I economic reconstruction period, European countries, their native unemployment still at a high rate, were reluctant to adopt permanently these thousands of aliens, most of whom were without guarantors or sponsors and were on the borderline of destitution. With no identity documents except, in some cases, a worthless Czarist passport, the refugees, even those few with the wherewithal to finance a journey, had no papers which would enable them legally to cross frontiers. Thus immobilized, living only by the sufferance of a foreign country, the refugees felt themselves an economic, and often social, embarrassment to their host nations. The countries which held large numbers of refugees were the very ones whose economies had received the roughest battering during the war, and their governments were reluctant to allocate funds for assistance. Private organizations which had been supplying emergency aid were finding it increasingly difficult to obtain continuing contributions for refugee aid.

The problem was laid in the lap of the League of Nations. In February 1921, with the endorsement of the League's member nations, the International Committee of the Red Cross and the League of Red Cross Societies made a formal request to the Council of the League of Nations to appoint a High Commissioner to "define the status of refugees" and "coordinate measures for their assistance." On 1 September 1921, the League appointed as High Commissioner Fridtjof Nansen of Norway.

At the first assembly of the League of Nations in 1920, Nansen was the head of the Norwegian delegation. He remained one of the outstanding members of the assembly until his death. In April 1920, before the formal establishment of the Office of the High Commissioner for Refugees, the League's council asked Nansen to take on the task of arranging repatriation from Russia of half a million prisoners of war from the former German and Austro-Hungarian armies. The Soviets did not recognize the League but did agree to negotiate with Nansen personally. In September 1922, he reported to the League that his efforts were successful: 427,886 prisoners had been repatriated. During this time Nansen had been campaigning for an identification document for displaced persons, a document which would be recognized by League member states and would permit displaced persons to move across borders. In July 1922, an international agreement was signed in Geneva which provided for an identification certificate which was to become known as the Nansen passport. The passport would be prepared by the High Commissioner's office and endorsed by the government of the country in which the displaced person or refugee had asylum. This was the first acknowledgement that refugees were entitled to recognition and respectability.

While the Nansen certificate was intended to be a temporary substitute for a national passport, it lacked the basic essential which made a national passport valuable to the holder: the right to return to the nation of issuance. Later, some of the League's member nations did endorse the certificate with a stipulation of this right, but this was not a universal practice. And, despite Nansen's appeals, the validity of the certificate was limited to one year, to be extended only with the concurrence of the country in which the refugee was quartered. The certificate was available only to Russian refugees and it did, in most cases, give its holder some advantage—the chances of obtaining a visa to another country, while not guaranteed, were greatly increased.

Nansen's organization then began work on relocating the refugees from congested—and often hostile—areas to places where they had some hope of a future. France and Germany accepted large numbers. A small number requested repatriation to Russia and, after Nansen received a guarantee from the Soviets that no reprisals would be undertaken, were returned. The remainder were located in forty-five countries. The United States, not a member of the League, took in several thousand families under its quota system.

For most of the Russian refugees, the only employment they could find in their new homelands was as manual laborers, a situation which created considerable hardship and distress among intellectuals.

But not all the Russian refugees were assisted by Nansen's office. Nearly one hundred thousand, mostly members of the White Army and their families, fled to Harbin and other cities in Manchuria. Some integrated themselves into the economy and about thirty thousand eventually managed to get down to Shanghai. It was not until 1946 and 1947, through the efforts of U.N. agencies and private relief agencies, that a small number of the surviving refugees and some of their children were able to leave. There is no record of the others.

As the resettlement efforts on behalf of the Russian refugees were coming to a close, the League's Office of the High Commissioner for Refugees tackled a new problem—the Armenian refugees.

The history of Armenia and the Armenians has been traced back to the seventh century before Christ. The country's boundaries have contracted and expanded throughout history and its population has shifted accordingly, but the Armenian region is generally considered to comprise what is today the Armenian Soviet Socialistic Republic, in the extreme southern portion of European Russia, and a contiguous area of approximately fifty thousand square miles of northeastern Turkey.

When World War I broke out, Turkey allied itself with Germany and Austria in the fight against the Western powers and Russia. In 1915, the Turks decided that the Armenians, many of whom had relatives in the Russian army, were a dangerous foreign element and set about deporting the entire population of about 1,750,000 to Syria and Mesopotamia, then part of Turkey's Ottoman Empire. The operation was carried out with ruthless barbarity. Approximately one-third of the Armenian population was massacred en route, another one-third managed to escape. The remainder did finally arrive in Syria and Mesopotamia (now Iraq). The Armenians living in Constantinople (Istanbul) and Smyrna (Izmir) were, initially, permitted to remain. After the 1918 Armistice, Constantinople was occupied by the French and Smyrna by the Greeks. In 1920 the allied powers recognized an independent Armenian government by the Treaty of Sèvres. Turkey was a cosignatory to the treaty. But in 1922, Turkey repudiated the treaty and invaded the Armenian nation, perpetrating wide-scale massacres as Turkish troops moved into the area. Then Turkish troops sacked Smyrna and massacred much of the Armenian and Greek population. Meanwhile the French had drawn down their forces in Constantinople. From Armenia and from areas in Turkey, Armenians, fearing death, left their homes.

When the League of Nations Council in February 1924 authorized the High Commissioner for Refugees to help alleviate the plight of the Armenians, their number was 320,000. In addition to those who had managed to reach Syria and Iraq, others found temporary haven in Palestine,

Cyprus, Bulgaria, Greece, and Western European countries. The League of Nations had little funds to allocate to help the Armenian refugees, but the British Lord Mayors' Fund contributed one hundred thousand pounds and contributions from private agencies in the United States provided an additional ten million dollars. In May 1924, Nansen received authorization from the League to issue Nansen certificates to the Armenian refugees.

Although the League was unsuccessful in obtaining contributions from member countries for the hapless Armenians, the League assembly did vote fifty thousand Swiss francs to finance the work of a commission of enquiry which would obtain information from the refugees as to their preferences for resettlement. The great majority opted to migrate to the new Soviet Armenian Republic. The Soviet government, while willing to accept the refugees, was unwilling to provide any funds for travel and settlement expenses. Dr. Nansen then issued an appeal to all the member states of the League for contributions. Only nine governments answered, and of these, five refused outright, and the other four made noncommittal replies. A second, stronger, appeal brought one affirmative reply. That was from Albania. Its offer: one thousand francs.

Once again, private organizations came to the rescue with funds, material, and manpower. By 1928, the Armenian refugees were dispersed throughout forty countries. Some one hundred thousand were settled in French-mandated Syria, at the initiative and with the cooperation of the French government.

In May 1930, Dr. Nansen died, his death mourned by friends of refugees all over the world. His last recommendation before his death was that assistance to refugees should be made a permanent part of the work of the League of Nations. But Nansen was not able to see the granting of his greatest wish.

With the passing of Nansen, the refugee activities of the League of Nations were reorganized. The post of high commissioner was abolished and the League Assembly established the Nansen International Office for Refugees. As with the high commission, only administrative funds were allocated to the office. The League, on the assumption that all major refugee problems would be solved by 1938, specified that the office would be liquidated by that time.

The crystal ball of the League, however, was more than slightly cloudy. The economic depression, with its high rate of unemployment, brought labor legislation which had the effect of denying refugees the right to work. By 1931, only a few countries were honoring the guarantees they had made when they signed the Nansen certificate pledges. Others simply refused to reendorse the certificates and, on the expiration of the certificate, ordered the refugees out of the country. Those who refused to leave were thrown in prison for violation of immigration laws.

In 1932, the League of Nations mandate over Iraq, the former Turkish province of Mesopotamia administered by Great Britain, ended and the Kingdom of Iraq came into being. In August 1933, an Iraqi army unit massacred over three hundred Assyrians, nearly the entire population of the village of Simail. The episode was applauded by most Iraqis and was not punished. This was followed by the flight of a large part of the hapless Assyrian community to Syria. Some twenty-five thousand refugees came across the border. Syria asked the Nansen office for aid, and a camp was set up in that country. A request for funds to feed and provide housing for the refugees was denied by the member countries.

In 1933, Hitler came to power in Germany and began to put into effect the plans he had outlined in *Mein Kampf,* which he had written years earlier. In 1935, the infamous Nuremberg decrees were enacted. Hitler's intention, set out repeatedly in *Mein Kampf,* was to annihilate all the Jews in Germany, and the Nazi administration adopted a two-phase program to eliminate the Jews. During the first phase, from 1933 to 1938, all Jewish businesses were "Aryanized," i.e., nationalized or taken over with little or no compensation by non-Jews, usually Nazi party members. Persons "polluted" with Jewish blood (those with at least one Jewish grandparent) were expelled from government positions. Jews had a special legal code applied to them. Later, all Jews were deprived of citizenship.

German Jews began to leave their country immediately after Hitler's advent to power. Some were those who had read, or heard of, Hitler's ideas about "creating a pure, Nordic race" and the "need for Aryanization"; they feared the worst. Others left at the urging of relatives in foreign countries who had a better perspective on German events than those inside Germany. The exodus increased monthly through 1933. In September of that year, the Dutch delegate to the League reported on the increasing numbers of Jews leaving Germany. The emphasis was on imbalances in the labor market resulting from the influx while only mildly criticizing the Nazi treatment of the Jews. Shortly thereafter, the League, over the noisy objection of the German delegation, authorized creation of a High Commission for Refugees

Coming From Germany. The office existed for three years, unable to function effectively for lack of funds.

In 1935, the Nansen office, which was not empowered to help the German Jews, was given responsibility for a new group of refugees—those from the Saarland. Largely inhabited by a German-speaking population but partially ruled by France from the time of the treaty of Westphalia in 1648 to the defeat of Napoleon, the Saarland was part of Germany from that time until the Treaty of Versailles after World War I. Under the treaty the rich Saar coal mines were ceded to France. In 1920, the area was placed under a governing commission of the League of Nations for 15 years, at the end of which time a plebiscite was to be held giving the inhabitants a choice of France, Germany, or maintenance of the status quo. When Hitler took over in Germany, one of his first acts was to inaugurate an intensive Nazi propaganda campaign in the Saarland. When the plebiscite was held in January 1935, more than 90 percent of the votes were for unification with Germany. The Saar was formally returned to the Reich on 1 March 1935, an event that marked the beginning of German expansion under Hitler. Two weeks later, Hitler denounced the clauses of the Versailles treaty providing for German disarmament. France, England, and Italy made diplomatic protests but took no further action. Nazi officials and party organizers then moved into the Saarland. A number of the inhabitants, particularly those who voted for reunion with France and who feared that their secret ballots might not have been secret, began to leave the area for France. The French delegation to the League asked that the Saar refugees be placed under the protection of the Nansen office. Nansen certificates were issued to the refugees and a special grant was made by the League assembly for resettlement of the refugees in Paraguay.

While the League was able to obtain a grant from the assembly to help resettle the Saarlanders, it was not able to provide more than token assistance to refugees being created in other areas. In Italy, as Mussolini tightened his grip and Fascist hoodlums were permitted, often encouraged, to persecute noncomformers, nearly a million persons were expelled from, or fled, Italy. In October 1935, Il Duce's troops invaded Ethiopia and in May 1936, Italy formally annexed that African country. Several thousand refugees, mainly from Addis Ababa, were added to the growing world total.

In July 1936, the civil war began in Spain and soon served as a theater of conflict for ideologies. To aid Franco's insurgents, Germany sent some ten thousand volunteers, most of whom were trained in aviation and tank warfare. Italy supplied between fifty and seventy thousand infantry and alpine troops. To support the Loyalists, Russia supplied armament and advisers. By the time the war had ended in March 1939, some half million Loyalist refugees had crossed the border into France. Additional thousands crossed when the Loyalists capitulated to the Fascists. Except for France, there was a general lack of compassion in the European countries concerning the situation of these Spanish refugees.

Appeals, of course, were made to the League of Nations. But the member nations, not wishing to incur the displeasure of Mussolini and Franco by giving aid to their opponents, denied the appeals of the high commissioner for funds to aid the new crop of refugees. Nor did any of the countries wish to appear to take sides in what some considered a proxy war between Germany and the Soviet Union.

From 1936 to 1938, the number of Jews leaving Germany mounted steadily. Unfortunately, most of the refugees went to countries which were eventually annexed by Hitler. Those who sought refuge in France, Holland, and Belgium were forced to take flight once more as the German armies pushed south and west. Going from border to border as stateless persons, they had difficulty in obtaining residence permits in any hoped-for country of asylum. Of those German Jews who fled eastward—to Poland, the Baltic countries, and Czechoslovakia—the great majority were picked up in the German blitzkreig and consigned to the ovens.

In Austria, following the *anschluss* of 1938, news of the concentration camps and extermination centers began to spread. More and more Jews cast about for escape from the Nazi holocaust. But again, country after country turned its back. Tens of thousands of refugees were turned away to suffer gassing and cremation because of deliberate red tape, stubborn bureaucracy, legal technicalities, and cold-blooded disinterest.

In September 1938, the League merged the High Commission for Refugees Coming From Germany, which had been sorrowfully impotent, with the Nansen office. But the new organization, the High Commission for Refugees, as with its predecessors, could do little for the Jews without support of member states.

Nor was there any significant aid from nonmember states. In the United States, repeated attempts to revise the immigration act were frustrated by Congress. Under the Immigration Act of 1924, which formalized an earlier quota system, quotas were allocated on the basis of the national origin of the population of the United States according to the census of 1920. Aliens seeking entry into the United States were divided into three categories: Asians, who were declared racially ineligible for citizenship and barred from permanent admission; those born in Western Hemisphere countries who could come in without any quota limitations; and all others who were assigned a numerical limit based on their country of birth. In this way, immigration from Northern and Western Europe was encouraged and from the southern and eastern parts discouraged.

Since the largest number of Americans in 1920 were of Anglo-Saxon descent, the United Kingdom was given the largest quota. Germany, Austria, Poland, and Czechoslovakia—all heavily populated with Jews—were provided only a small fraction of quotas in proportion to the numbers who wished to flee. The United States Congress, despite constant prodding by President Roosevelt and the Department of State, refused to enlarge, or reallocate the unused portion of, the quotas from these countries. While in the United States one hundred thousand quota numbers per year were being forfeited, Jews were being incinerated in the ovens of Auschwitz, Buchenwald, Dachau, and other extermination centers.

In February 1938, President Roosevelt, shocked by the reports of Nazi atrocities, sent a message to thirty-two nations asking them to attend an international conference to discuss resettlement possibilities for German Jews. Nearly all the Latin American countries attended, plus Australia, Belgium, the United Kingdom, Canada, Denmark, France, Ireland, the Netherlands, New Zealand, Norway, Sweden, Switzerland, and the United States. The conference was held at Évian-les-Bains, France, a spa on the southern shore of Lake Geneva.

When the conference opened in July 1938, the skies over the southern end of Lake Geneva were cloudy, an unusual condition for that time of the year. The dark heavens were a portent of what was to be the result of the conference. The positions of the United Kingdom and France set a pattern for the rest of the delegations. Lord Winterton, the British delegate, stated that his government could not permit Jewish resettlement in British-mandated Palestine (the Balfour Declaration of 1917 stated that "nothing shall be done which may prejudice the civil and religious rights of existing non-Jewish communities in Palestine."). As for the United Kingdom itself, Lord Winterton said, "it is not a country of immigration . . ." The French delegate, in eloquent Gallic phrases, pointed out that his country was in complete agreement with the principle of aiding refugees, but that unfortunately France's zeal to serve the cause of humanity was conditioned by its lack of resources. Other European countries excused themselves on the grounds that a relaxation of immigration strictures would result in an influx of refugees to such an extent that economic dislocation would result. Phrases like "undue economic competition" and "expanding unemployment" were tacked on to statements about the impossibility of changing laws.

The Latin American countries, with the exception of the Dominican Republic which agreed to accept one hundred thousand refugees, stated they had pressing unemployment problems. Most of these countries also noted that they had trade agreements with the Reich and didn't want to take any action which would bring on German displeasure and thus risk loss of their trade.

Although the United States had initiated the conference, the U.S. delegate was in no position to state that Congress would relax the immigration laws, the key to any plan to relocate refugees in the United States.

The conference was a failure. Activities in Auschwitz, Bergen-Belsen, Buchenwald, and a dozen other centers were stepped up.

At the United Nations meeting on Refugees and Displaced Persons in Southeast Asia held in Geneva in July 1979, Vice President Walter Mondale referred to the Évian meeting: "Forty-one years ago this very week, thirty-two nations of asylum convened at Évian to save the doomed Jews of Germany. At Évian, they began with high hopes, but they failed the test of civilization. The civilized world hid in the cloak of legalism."

The representatives at the Évian conference did, however, decide to set up the Intergovernmental Committee for Refugees, composed of the countries represented at the conference. The IGCR would explore "resettlement opportunities" and try to find a substitute for the "existing disorderly exodus of men, women, and children who have no definite place to go."

The creation of the IGCR did little to dispel the prevailing international apathy toward the situation of the refugees. Germany, which of course refused to recognize the legitimacy of the IGCR, continued to create refugees. When, as a result of the Munich agreements of 1938 (which were to lead to "peace in our time"), the Nazis began to dismember Czechoslovakia, many Czechs fled.

In April 1939, the Italians, taking advantage of the confusion produced by the German absorption of Czechoslovakia, invaded Albania. Some three thousand Albanians fled across the border into Yugoslavia. When Germany invaded Poland in September 1939, some three hundred thousand Poles sought sanctuary in the Soviet Union.

With the German drives into Belgium, the Netherlands, Luxembourg, and northern France, five million refugees moved down to southern France (only to be overrun when the Germans extended their occupation to all of France in November 1942). With the campaign against the Balkan countries, another three hundred thousand refugees were on the run, and one hundred thousand of these were candidates for the crematoria.

In Northern Europe, a new crop of refugees was in the making. The first war between the Soviet Union and Finland began on 30 November 1939. Known as the Winter War, it ended on 12 March 1940, when the Finns were forced to sign a treaty with the Soviets. Under the terms of the treaty, Finland lost the entire Karelian Isthmus and an area around Lake Ladoga. The treaty permitted the inhabitants of the area to leave or remain under Soviet rule: 99 percent of the population, some 415,000 persons, were evacuated into Finland.

In June 1941, Finland joined Germany in the invasion of the Soviet Union. The Finnish troops quickly recaptured most of the lost territory, and in August of 1941 the original evacuees began a return movement. Within the next twenty-four months, some 265,000 persons of the original 415,000 had moved back to their original homeland and started to rebuild their homes, most of which had been destroyed in the war. When Finland signed the peace treaty in Paris in February 1947, she had to cede the Karelian territory to the Soviets. Finland had to reabsorb more than 420,000 refugees, most of whom had left the area originally in 1940 and had returned in 1941 or 1942.

The tragic story of the ordeal of the European Jews in the immediate prewar and war years is familiar to the Western world. Before World War II the Jews of Europe constituted the intellectual and cultural center of world Jewry. By the end of the war, of the some six and one half million European Jews outside the Soviet Union, fewer than two million survived. Of the approximately three million Russian Jews, fewer than two million were alive. Of the three million Jews in Poland, only four hundred and fifty thousand survived.

The few efforts made by the IGCR were met with a lack of response on the part of its member countries. The organization, however, was able to conclude a few minor immigration agreements with three Latin American nations. The Soviet Union, as anticipated, consistently refused to participate in any proposal to provide resettlement opportunities to refugees from the Soviet dominated areas.

In November 1943, the forty-four nations which had declared war on Germany signed the charter of a new international organization, the United Nations Relief and Rehabilitation Administration. UNRRA had its origins in a proposal made by the British to the United States in 1943 that thought be given to some sort of "Allied Post-War Requirements Bureau." The idea was supported by the United States and several other governments. The organization's task would be the reconstruction of devastated areas and the provisioning of relief food, clothing, and medical supplies to the needy nationals of the U.N. countries, and the repatriation of refugees.

But on the subject of refugees, UNRRA's General Council found that it could not arrive at a modus operandi that would be satisfactory to all the member states. Further, there was lack of agreement as to definitions and classes of refugees.

In January 1944, frustrated by lack of international action, President Roosevelt issued an executive order establishing the War Refugee Board of the United States, which was directed to "rescue the victims of enemy oppression who are in imminent danger of death . . ." The Board rescued approximately fifty thousand Jews from concentration camps by buying their lives through the Swiss government and voluntary agencies operating from Switzerland. But by the end of 1944, the Germans discontinued acceptance of ransom for the victims.

IX

A Review of Refugees around the World—1945 and Beyond

When the Second World War came to an end in Europe in May 1945, the United Nations Relief and Rehabilitation Agency had already been active in repatriation work and aiding, to a considerable extent, in resettling refugees in other countries. But since UNRRA's terms of reference did not include resettlement work, it was unable to solve the problem (i.e., finding them new homes in countries willing to accept them) of the last million remaining refugees living in European camps by the end of 1946. The Intergovernmental Committee for Refugees, whose concern the last million refugees was supposed to be, was without funds or support. At the first session of the United Nations General Assembly in London in January 1946, the subject of refugees and displaced persons was discussed, but no formal action was taken. Eventually, however, the discussions and arguments in the United Nation's Special Committee on Refugees and Displaced Persons led to the birth of the International Refugee Organization. Although the IRO had been established as a temporary organization, its life was extended more than once.

A survey of the many programs, organizations, agencies, and committees established on national and international levels which were formed to help refugees at various times and in various countries would make a book in itself. Our theme here, however, concerns the people themselves. In May 1948, a new outburst of violence occurred in the Middle East. With the formal ending of the British mandate of Palestine, the Arab population did everything in its power to abort the birth of the new nation of Israel. After months of bloody fighting, the Israelis prevailed. Nearly a million Arab refugees crossed the borders into Jordan, Lebanon, Iraq, Syria, and Gaza. Later, finding that the Israelis were not intent on reprisals, many of these refugees moved, or were moved, back to Israel. A separate United Nations organ, the U.N. Relief and Works Agency for Palestine Refugees in the Near East (UNRWA), which was established to deal with this problem, is still operating. At the end of 1979, more than a million and a half Palestinian refugees were registered with UNRWA. According to a 1979 estimate by the Congressional Research Service of the Library of Congress, there are between three and a half and four million refugees in the Middle East.

The situation of the Palestinian refugees and the continuing Arab pressure on Israel has been a volatile political issue from the day of the founding of the Jewish state. Another complicated situation, but on a smaller scale, exists with the Kurds in the Middle East. The Kurds are a non-Arab Muslim people living in several Middle Eastern countries. In most of these they are a mistreated minority. Iraqi Kurds are refugees in Iran, and Iranian Kurds are refugees in Iraq.

As with UNRWA, another U.N. agency operated in an area not assigned as an UNHCR responsibility—the United Nations Korean Reconstruction Agency (UNKRA). Established in 1951, it conducts relief operations, including the care of displaced persons, in Korea. When the Korean truce was signed on 27 July 1953, more than five million refugees were in the Republic of Korea. Today all of these have been resettled and the South Korean government provides whatever assistance is required to these persons.

On 23 October 1956, the Hungarian Revolution began. Fighting in the streets of Budapest went on until 30 October, when the Russians pulled their tanks out of the city. On 3 November, three Russian generals arrived in Budapest to begin talks with Hungarian officials on the "logistical and technical aspects" of Soviet troop withdrawal. The talks began at ten in the morning and were recessed from noon until nine in the evening of the same day. Shortly after midnight, a Russian in a Red Army uniform without insignia joined the group. He spoke to the Hungarian officials, "You are all under arrest." The man was Ivan Serov, head of the KGB, the Soviet secret police. His men had surrounded the meeting place. Two hours later, at 3 A.M. 4 November, Soviet tanks rolled into Budapest. In the next few days, thousands of persons were arrested, hundreds of university students were hanged. Journalists, well known writers, and other "misguided intellectuals" were taken to police stations, questioned, and beaten. Some were released, some imprisoned, others clubbed to death.

Earlier, on 28 October, the Austrian government had announced it would grant asylum to all refugees. In the first week after the announcement, some 10,000 Hungarians, mostly peasants and residents of border villages, crossed the border. With the return of the Russian tanks to Budapest, a massive exodus began. Every class of the population, individuals and entire families, the old and the young, from every part of Hungary, fled to Austria and Yugoslavia. By 28 November, 90,000 Hungarians had crossed into Austria. In the course of the next three months, another 70,000 sought refuge in that country. By the end of July 1957, more than 200,000 Hungarians had become refugees. Some 180,000 had fled to Austria, 20,000 to Yugoslavia.

The Austrians provided transportation from the border, accommodation, and food. But the Austrian government was not able to cope with the increasing flow of refugees and on 4 November appealed to the UNHCR and the ICEM. There was an immediate outside response to this newest refugee crisis. Western European countries sent planes, trains, and buses to Austria to bring back refugees to their countries. The French Red Cross, on 7 November, flew a transport plane loaded with medical supplies to Austria and flew back with a planeload of refugees who accepted the invitation to settle in France. A number of British private organizations, and later commercial aircraft companies, shuttled planes between the United Kingdom and Austria, bringing in thousands of refugees. Switzerland sent a special train. Buses from Sweden and trains from Belgium and the Netherlands shuttled back and forth. Governments and voluntary agencies responded quickly and generously. As more aid, both monetary and material, poured in and as additional voluntary agencies and church groups set up functioning offices in Vienna, the Austrian government called upon the UNHCR to coordinate overall operations.

By 1 March 1958, 154,073 refugees had departed Austria, approximately one-half for overseas and one-half to Western European countries.

The total number of refugees who had fled to Yugoslavia numbered 19,857. The Yugoslav government at first provided accommodation, food, and other assistance without outside aid. But, as the influx increased, the Yugoslavs requested assistance from UNHCR. By the end of January 1958, some 16,000 refugees were resettled in other countries, 675 chose to remain in Yugoslavia, and the rest chose voluntary repatriation (by this time the Hungarian government had announced that no reprisals would be taken against those who had fled the country).

The Hungarian experience made an indelible impression on the democratic countries. They realized that the refugee problem was one likely to continue, in one form or another, in one area or another. It also was clear that the countries of first asylum could not be expected to cope with the burden alone. But the experience proved that a refugee problem could be met by an immediate and organized resettlement program, and particularly by multinational sympathy and compassion manifested, not only by financial aid, but also by acceptance of the unfortunate human beings.

The Hungarian crisis also demonstrated the need for a permanent international organization for dealing with refugee situations. And it showed that the voluntary agencies, national and international, had a crucial role to play in the operational aspects of relief and resettlement.

In the United States, the Hungarian refugees were looked upon as heroes, and the American people gave them a warm welcome. The positive reaction in the press and on the radio and television was undoubtedly the prime factor in creating support for the refugees. A wire service photo of Hungarian teenagers throwing rocks at a Russian tank was printed in 75 percent of American newspapers.

Thus the action taken by the United States was immediate. The first 5,000 Hungarians were admitted under the provisions of an amendment to the Refugee Relief Act of 1953. Then, responding to the continuing buildup of the refugees in Austrian camps, the president authorized entry of an additional 16,500 Hungarians. By the time the flow had stopped, some 30,000 Hungarian refugees had been settled in the United States.

Since Hungary, the displacement of human beings has proceeded apace. At the beginning of 1980, estimates of the world's permanently unsettled population ranged from ten million to thirteen million. Every country, in one way or another, has been affected. And the numbers of refugees are increasing.

Since its founding the UNHCR has salvaged more than twenty million homeless people uprooted because of invasions, occupations, wars, famines, and political, ethnic, and religious persecution. In the United States, the results of our refugee policy since the end of World War II have been satisfactory to all except a small body of ultraconservatives who see the country as being overrun by foreigners. But the great majority of refugees who have settled in our fifty states have made a good adjustment to their new surroundings. Offered a fair chance by the people of the community in which they settle, they usually succeed, and instead of a problem the refugees become an asset in their adoptive communities.

Authors' Note

The authors of this book have long maintained interest in Asia, particularly Southeast Asia which has served as the setting of previous books and which has been the locale for both military and civilian pursuits dating back to 1949. Over the years we have observed the continuing appreciation of Asian thought, philosophy, and outlook, as well as the increasing impact of Asia on the politics and economics of the rest of the world. Happily, the world's attention, which once looked almost exclusively to the West for innovations in contemporary thought and action, no longer excludes Asia. The varied and colorful peoples of the Orient have come into their own, and in spite of continuing suspicion, distrust, and conflict, the Asian milieu has become a legitimate and provocative field of study for scholars of many disciplines.

Long before this happened, some writers, reporters, and other observers were talking about the potential of this area, so rich in manpower and resources. Today they are seeing their predictions come true, their warnings being borne out, and their particular field of expertise invaded by other researchers. We are sure they are gratified. In their footsteps came other journalists, doctoral candidates, and the plain curious, who have been snared in the intangible, elusive, and unbreakable web of Asia.

In the beginning of this book we ask who can know the heart and mind of Indochina? Here is a list of people who know a lot, and their works. To them we express our gratitude for supplementing our understanding and for providing us with much pleasure. Highly recommended are:

Southeast Asia by Tillman Durdin, Atheneum, New York, 1966; *An Eye for the Dragon, Southeast Asia Observed, 1954–1970* by Dennis Bloodworth, Farrar, Straus, and Giroux, New York, 1970; *A History of Southeast Asia* by D.G.E. Hall, MacMillan, London, 1964; *Thailand, Burma, Laos* and *Cambodia* by John F. Cady, Prentice-Hall, Englewood Cliffs, N.J., 1966; *Vietnam: A Political History* by Joseph Buttinger, Frederick A. Praeger, New York & Washington, 1968; *Southeast Asia* by Stanley Karnow and the editors of *Life,* Time-Life Books, New York, 1967; *The Mekong, River of Terror and Hope* by Peter T. White, National Geographic, Washington, 1968; *The Montagnards of South Vietnam* by Robert L. Mole, Charles E. Tuttle Co., Japan, 1970; *Fire in the Lake* by Frances Fitzgerald, Atlantic-Little, Brown, Boston, Toronto, 1972; *On the Other Side* by Kate Webb, Quadrangle Books, New York, 1972; and *The Scrutable East* by Robert Trumbull, David McKay, New York, 1964.

Appendix 1

United States Policy and the Refugee

The attitudes of the American public—and official United States policy—towards refugees have ranged from mistrust to sympathy during the two hundred plus years we have been a nation.

When our country was founded, its citizens were, in large part, refugees, sons and daughters or grandsons and granddaughters of refugees themselves. The United States, by not having a formalized immigration policy, had in effect decided on an open-door policy—any alien who could manage to reach our shores was free to enter the country. There was no distinction between immigrant and refugee. Europeans fleeing the revolutions of 1830 and 1848, and the Irish leaving because of the potato famine received the same treatment—and welcome—as any other foreigner entering the country.

In 1875, Congress passed the country's first immigration act, which established admission criteria for the immigrants. Again no distinction was made between immigrant and refugee—if a person met the admission criteria he was admitted; if not, he was excluded. Jewish refugees from the Russian pogroms which occurred from 1811 to 1917 were accepted as other immigrants.

The first reference in any U.S. immigration law to persons who could be classified as refugees came in 1917 legislation; it required literacy tests of most immigrants, but exempted persons fleeing religious persecution from this requirement.

In 1921, the United States enacted the first of its country-of-origin quota laws, which set numerical limits on the numbers of immigrants from specific countries of origin. The quotas in the 1921 law were allocated on the basis of the national origins of the residents of the United States indicated in the 1920 census. Thus it was easy for potential immigrants from Northern and Western European countries to enter but quite difficult for those from Eastern and Southern Europe.

That part of Emma Lazarus' sonnet, "The New Colossus," which is inscribed on the pedestal of the Statue of Liberty:

> Give me your tired, your poor,
> Your huddled masses, yearning to breathe free,
> The wretched refuse of your teeming shore,
> Send these, the homeless, the tempest-tossed, to me:
> I lift my lamp beside the golden door.

applied only if you came from the right country.

At the end of the war in Europe in May 1945, there were an estimated 30 million displaced persons. The private voluntary agencies in America, which were pressing for a change in the law covering admission of these refugees, worked out an understanding with the U.S. State Department and the Immigration and Naturalization Service which resulted in the Truman Directive of December 1945. While Congress held on to the ethnocentric country-of-origin system for allocating immigrant visas, the Truman Directive permitted admission of displaced persons, under existing quotas, by giving preference to refugees over nonrefugees. The voluntary agencies guaranteed that they would meet the costs of resettlement and see to it that none of the refugees became public charges.

From the time of the Truman Directive until 1965, a number of executive and legislative acts provided for admission of more refugees without any change in the country-of-origin system. The Displaced Persons Act of 1948, the Refugee Relief Act of 1953, and the Refugee-Escape Act of 1957 all provided short-term exceptions to the basic law, permitting entry of refugees who otherwise would not be admissible. Additionally, American presidents, acting through their attorneys general, would utilize their powers as administrators of the law, to parole refugees into the nation.

The parole authority permitted a person to enter the country as a parolee, or as a conditional entrant, and then, without leaving the country, adjust his status to that of an immigrant. Generally refugees must wait for two years in a parole status before applying for adjustment. (However, there was special legislation enacted for the Hungarians in 1958, the Cubans in 1966, and the Indochinese in 1977 which provided automatic immigrant status after two years without regard to numerical limitations.)

The country-of-origin visa allocation system was finally repealed in 1965. The United States, for the first time, wrote into continuing legislation provisions for acceptance of refugees as such. The 1965 amendments to the immigration law provided for the conditional entry of 10,200 refugees. This number was increased to 17,400 in 1978 amendments; it was reserved for refugees who fled from Communist countries or the Middle East because of persecution, and for those who were the victims of natural disasters. These allocations have been filled each year by refugees from the Eastern European countries, some Chinese who came out through Hongkong, and Kurds, Jews, and Arabs from the Middle East.

When the first mass exodus of Vietnamese occurred, the perceptions and attitudes of the American people toward them did not augur well for a warm welcome. America's long and frustrating military involvement in Vietnam was undoubtedly largely responsible for an initial feeling of indifference —even hostility in some quarters—towards the refugees. A Gallup poll taken in May 1975 indicated that Americans were opposed to admitting Vietnamese refugees by 54 percent to 36 percent. A front-page article in the 22 May 1975 issue of *The Wall Street Journal,* ''Vietnamese Refugees Find Starting Anew is a Frustrating Ordeal,'' cited the high unemployment rate (8.9 percent) in the United States, the tremendous language barrier, the above cited Gallup poll, and insufficient government follow-up as factors that would substantially work against effective resettlement efforts.

Congressional reaction in May and June 1975 was also mixed. Substantial concern was expressed about health and employment issues and the fiscal impact of so many refugees on American communities. Despite these reservations by some members of Congress, the Judiciary committees of both houses moved very quickly with the administration to design new refugee legislation which was enacted on 22 May 1975. The Indochina Migration and Refugee Assistance Act authorized a massive federal role in reception and resettlement for a period of two years. A total of $505 million was made available for the first year, about $98 million in AID funds by presidential determination, $305 million appropriated to the State Department, and $100 million to HEW. Over half of the money, some $275 million, was spent on evacuation of the refugees and the operation of reception centers overseas and in the United States. Approximately $75 million was allocated to the voluntary agencies and other State Department-funded domestic activities, while $153 million (including $53 million transferred from remaining State Department funds) was channeled through the Department of Health, Education, and Welfare.

Yet the majority of the refugees who have entered the United States in recent years have done so under various special refugee programs authorized on behalf of persons who are not eligible under the existing refugee provision because of its ideological, geographic, or numerical limitations.

In 1979, Congress began work on major refugee reform legislation designed to establish a comprehensive policy on refugee admission and assistance. Emphasis is on development of a policy which would have a permanent statutory basis, but which would be flexible enough to be responsive to unforeseen emergency refugee situations.

The act would eliminate the present conditional entry provision, replacing it with new provisions for the regular admission of refugees and their admission in emergency situations.

The act would also eliminate the ideological and geographic limitations of the present definition of refugee, so that it would conform with the broader definition used in the United Nations Protocol and Convention Relating to the Status of Refugees. Since 1968, the United States has been a party to the 1967 United Nations Protocol Relating to the Status of Refugees, which incorporates by reference provisions of the 1951 United Nations Convention Relating to the Status of Refugees. The protocol and convention are designed to assure fair and humane treatment for any person who, owing to persecution or a well-founded fear of persecution on account of race, religion, nationality, membership of a particular social group, or political opinion, is unable or unwilling to return to his country of nationality or residence.

Distinctions between the U.S. definition and that of the United Nations were essentially geographic and ideological. The definition of refugee adopted by the United Nations is:

Any person, who owing to a well-founded fear of being persecuted for reasons of race, religion, nationality or political opinion, is outside the country of his nationality and is unable or, owing to such fear or for reasons other than personal convenience, is unwilling to avail himself of the protection of that country; or, who not having a nationality and being outside the country of his normal habitual residence, is unable or, owing to such fear or for reasons other than personal convenience, is unwilling to return to it.

Under normal immigration procedures established by the legislation, up to fifty thousand refugees per year may be admitted to the United States for permanent residence. A number in excess of fifty thousand may be admitted if the president determines, after consultation with the House and Senate Judiciary committees, that an excess is warranted by humanitarian concerns or is otherwise in the national interest. Beginning in 1983, the total number of refugees to be admitted for permanent residence is determined by the president after consultation with the Judiciary committees. The president also determines the allocation of refugee admissions among refugee groups during a given fiscal year and is required to report anticipated allocations to the House and Senate Judiciary committees prior to the beginning of the fiscal year.

The president can determine, after consultation with the House and Senate Judiciary committees, that an emergency refugee situation exists and refugee admissions beyond those established for a given fiscal year be allocated on an emergency basis among refugees of special humanitarian concern to the United States.

Refugees would be admitted and be exempted from the Immigration and Nationality Act's exclusion provisions regarding labor certification, public charges, visas and documentation, literacy, and foreign medical graduates. The attorney general may waive some of the other exclusions in the interest of humanitarianism or to assure family unity.

All regular and emergency refugee admissions are in addition to the worldwide immigration ceiling set forth in the legislation as 270,000 visas per year. Those aliens granted asylum enter the United States on a conditional basis and may have their status adjusted after two years. The attorney general may use up to 5,000 of the annual refugee admissions to adjust the status of these aliens.

The Immigration and Nationality Act is amended by the legislation to make the withholding of an alien's deportation mandatory under certain conditions, such as danger of persecution, to bring this provision into accord with the United States' obligations under the United Nations Convention and Protocol Relating to the Status of Refugees.

The legislation precludes the attorney general from admitting refugees under his parole authority except under limited circumstances.

The legislation creates an Office of Refugee Resettlement within the Department of Health, Education, and Welfare, headed by a director appointed by the secretary, to administer all domestic assistance for refugees.

To receive assistance under the legislation, a state must submit a plan to the Director of the Office of Refugee Resettlement describing how it will deal with refugee resettlement in certain specific areas set forth in the bill. States must also report annually to the director on the uses of funds provided under the program.

Specific assistance authorized by the legislation includes initial resettlement grants and contracts for public or nonprofit private agencies; grants and contracts for services to refugees including those promoting economic self-sufficiency, English language training, and health services; assistance for refugee children including special education services, child welfare services, and maintenance payments for refugee children up to the first four years they are in the United States or, if accompanied by an adult, until they are eighteen years old; and 100 percent reimbursement to states for cash and medical assistance provided refugees for the first four years of their residence in the United States.

The United States had not developed a comprehensive policy concerning assistance provided to refugees upon their arrival in the United States, largely because of the unpredictable and emergency nature of refugee situations. Assistance to refugees in the United States has traditionally been provided by private, nonprofit voluntary agencies active in immigration and refugee affairs including religious and nonsectarian social service organizations. Whether federal assistance is provided to refugees, the nature of such assistance, and the duration of such refugee programs, are issues which were resolved on an ad hoc basis.

Under the new legislation the voluntary agencies will continue to play a vital role in assistance to the refugee. Since World War II the voluntary agencies have been the organizations in most direct contact with the refugees because they have assumed responsibility for the day-to-day premigration counseling, reception, placement, and other resettlement efforts. The agencies traditionally provided assistance without government support, using their own resources and volunteers to provide services to refugees. The Cuban, Soviet, and Indochinese programs, however, have been accompanied by per capita grants to the agencies, although this funding does not cover all the costs of resettlement.

The nonsectarian agencies have normally relied upon sponsorship of refugees by individuals or community groups or have taken on the assignment of sponsors directly, relying upon a network of local offices staffed by caseworkers. The agencies with a religious affiliation have normally linked refugees with their diocesan structures or local churches which provide direct services to refugees.

As of the beginning of 1980, there were four refugee programs in which the U.S. government provides funds for resettlement agencies. The State Department provides per capita resettlement grants for Indochinese refugees ($350) and Soviet, Eastern European, and other refugees ($250) in differing amounts. The Cuban placement programs, funded by HEW, are presently too small to justify a per capita system of fund allocations, but some small grants were made. The only matching grant program among the four is HEW's $1,000 per capita program for Eastern European refugees, which is primarily for Soviet Jews. The $1,000 grant covers long-term resettlement services rather than just the reception and placement expenses.

The largest of the resettlement agencies is the Migration and Refugee Services of the U.S. Catholic Conference, which operates as an arm of the Catholic Church. There are three Protestant resettlement agencies: the Lutheran Immigration and Refugee Service; the World Relief Services, a new entity among the resettlement agencies which relates to the Evangelical churches; and Church World Service, which works through other (non-Lutheran and non-Evangelical) Protestant churches.

HIAS (Hebrew Immigrant Aid Society) offers its assistance to refugees through a network of Jewish Family Service agencies. Rav Tov (Hebrew words meaning approximately "much good") is a newcomer to the field, specializing in the resettlement of religiously conservative Jews.

The Tolstoy Foundation was created earlier in this century to help White Russian refugees, particularly those in the arts. Today it provides assistance for all refugees from Soviet Russia.

The resettlement of the Soviet refugees is well-organized and extensive. HIAS is the most active of the voluntary agencies, resettling most of the Jewish refugees. HIAS relies on the Council of Jewish Federations to mobilize groups such as the New York Association for New Americans, the Jewish Family and Community Service in Chicago, and other Jewish family and community organizations in more than 150 cities across America. Private Jewish citizens have been most generous with financial contributions and the donation of their time in the resettlement effort.

The resettlement of the Kurds and the Chileans was accomplished almost entirely within the private sector. The voluntary agencies were active, though sometimes drawing mixed reviews. Amnesty International is not a resettlement agency, but in keeping with its focus on political prisoners has served as an advocate for the admission and resettlement of the Chileans. The Lutheran Immigration and Refugee Service (LIRS) also had a special interest in the Chileans because their church has been active in Chile, and its leaders there were deeply involved in seeking to help the political prisoners. Church World Service and the International Rescue Committee have also sponsored these refugees.

Much of the private sector's efforts on behalf of the Kurds and Chileans was the result of highly localized efforts, such as those of Father Moriarty's Roman Catholic Church of the Sacred Heart in San Jose, California; the Bay Area Program in San Francisco and Berkeley, California; and the Chilean Refugee Resettlement Program in Seattle, Washington. The existence of sympathetic communities with clusters of Chileans has shown that localized efforts such as these are extremely helpful, even necessary, in the resettlement process.

As this is being written, a massive influx of Cuban refugees is taking place. A new boat people, thousands and thousands, are streaming into Key West and other points in Florida. President Carter has invoked legislation which will provide the state of Florida with emergency funds to help assist these 1980 refugees.

Today, the American people are generally sympathetic to the plight of the refugees, whether Cuban, Indochinese, Russian, or Kurdish. And official U.S. policies, despite the fitful evolution of laws on refugees and immigrants, have reflected this sympathy.

Appendix 2

MEMORANDUM OF UNDERSTANDING BETWEEN THE GOVERNMENT OF THE SOCIALIST REPUBLIC OF VIET NAM AND THE OFFICE OF THE UNITED NATIONS HIGH COMMISSIONER FOR REFUGEES (UNHCR) CONCERNING THE DEPARTURE OF PERSONS FROM THE SOCIALIST REPUBLIC OF VIET NAM:

Following discussion held in Hanoi between representatives of the Government of the Socialist Republic of Viet Nam and a delegation of the Office of the United Nations High Commissioner for Refugees (UNHCR) from 26 February to 5 March and from 25 May to 30 May 1979, it is agreed that UNHCR will facilitate the implementation of the 12 January announcement by the Vietnamese Government to permit the orderly departure of persons who wish to leave Viet Nam for countries of new residence. Regarding the programme to implement such orderly departure, it is understood that:

    1. Authorized exit of those people who wish to leave Viet Nam and settle in foreign countries—family reunion and other humanitarian cases—will be carried out as soon as possible and to the maximum extent. The number of such people will depend both on the volume of applications for exit from Viet Nam and on receiving countries' ability to issue entry visas.

    2. The election of those people authorized to go abroad under this programme will, whenever possible, be made on the basis of the lists prepared by the Vietnamese Government and the lists prepared by the receiving countries. Those persons whose names appear on both lists will qualify for exit. As for those persons whose names appear on only one list, their cases will be subject to discussions between UNHCR and the Vietnamese Government or the Governments of the receiving countries as appropriate.

3.   UNHCR will make every effort to enlist support for this programme amongst potential receiving countries.

4.   The Vietnamese Government and UNHCR will each appoint personnel who will closely cooperate in the implementation of this programme.

5.   This personnel will be authorized to operate in Hanoi and Ho Chi Minh City, and as necessary, to go to other places to promote exit operations.

6.   Exit operations will be effected at regular intervals by appropriate means of transport.

7.   The Vietnamese Government will, subject to relevant Vietnamese laws, provide UNHCR and the receiving countries with every facility to implement this programme.

Appendix 3

**CONTRIBUTIONS TO UNHCR PROGRAMS
FOR INDOCHINESE REFUGEES**
**(Contributions pledged and/or paid for 1979,
including contributions in kind) (in U.S. dollars)**

AS OF SEPTEMBER 30, 1979

GOVERNMENTS

Australia	3,393,741
Austria	75,188
Canada	1,028,956
Canada (Provincial Govt. of Alberta)	854,701
China, People's Republic of	973,141
Denmark	1,889,466
Finland	1,000,000
Germany	6,166,037
Iran	90,000
Ireland	400,000
Israel	5,000
Italy	1,235,006
Japan	38,000,000
Netherlands	6,657,812
New Zealand	209,180
Norway	1,960,784
Papua New Guinea	300,000
Republic of Korea	5,000,000
Republic of South Africa	50,301
Spain	50,000

(continued)

Appendix 3 (continued)

Sweden	2,544,496
Switzerland	3,102,354
Tunisia	5,000
U.S.A.	41,500,000
TOTAL GOVERNMENTS	116,441,163
International Organizations:	
European Economic Community	31,236,678
Parliament of Europe	1,368,430
Sovereign Order of Malta	10,000
TOTAL GOVERNMENTS & INTERNATIONAL ORGANIZATIONS	149,056,271
Private and Other Sources	6,379,223
GRAND TOTAL	155,435,494

Appendix 4

UNHCR OPERATIONS AND ADMINISTRATIVE BUDGET
1979 Contributions

Donor	Millions of Dollars			
	General Program	Special Program	Total	%
U.S.A.	$12.5	$ 5.0	$17.5	19.8
Japan	11.6	0.1	11.7	13.2
United Kingdom	7.2	1.9	9.1	10.3
Sweden	6.4	1.6	8.0	9.0
Netherlands	4.7	2.8	7.5	8.5
Denmark	4.2	1.3	5.5	6.2
Germany, Federal Republic of	3.6	0.4	4.0	4.5
Norway	2.3	0.9	3.2	3.6
Canada	2.3	0.2	2.5	2.8
Switzerland	1.2	-0-	1.2	1.4
Australia	0.8	0.3	1.1	1.2
Saudi Arabia	1.0	-0-	1.0	1.1
France	0.7	-0-	0.7	0.8
Belgium	0.3	0.1	0.4	0.5
Finland	0.4	-0-	0.4	0.5
Rest of world (including European Economic Community)	8.8	5.9	14.7	16.6
Total	68.0	20.5	88.5	100.0

The UNHCR also received $22 million from the regular (assessed) U.N. budget in 1979.

Appendix 5

ORGANIZATIONS IN THE UNITED STATES WHICH WILL ACCEPT CONTRIBUTIONS FOR ASSISTANCE TO INDOCHINESE REFUGEES

American Friends Service Committee
1501 Cherry St.
Philadelphia PA 19102

American Baptist Churches
Board of International Ministries
Valley Forge PA 19481

American Jewish Joint
Distribution Committee
60 E. 42nd St.
New York NY 10017

American Red Cross National
Headquarters
17th and D. Sts. NW
Washington DC 20005

American Refugee Committee
310 Fourth Ave., South
Minneapolis MN 55415

C.A.R.E.
660 First Ave.
New York NY 10016

Catholic Relief Services
1011 First Ave.
New York NY 10022

Church World Service
475 Riverside Drive
New York NY 10027

International Catholic Migration
Commission
c/o U.S. Catholic Conference
1312 Massachusetts Ave. NW
Washington DC 20005

International Rescue Committee
386 Park Ave., South
New York NY 10016

Lutheran World Relief
360 Park Ave., South
New York NY 10010

Mennonite Central Committee
21 South 12th St.
Akron PA 17501   *(continued)*

Appendix 5 (continued)

Oxfam America
302 Columbus Ave.
Boston MA 02116

Save the Children
48 Wilton Road
Westport CT 06880

Seventh-Day Adventist World Service
6840 Eastern Ave. NW
Washington DC 20012

Southern Baptist Convention
Baptist World Alliance
628 Sixteenth St. N.W.
Washington, D.C. 20009

Synagogue Council of America
432 Park Ave. South
New York NY 10016

U.N. High Commissioner for Refugees
Region 9, Room C-301
U.N. Plaza
New York NY 10017

U.S. Committee for UNICEF
331 E. 38th St.
New York NY 10016

World Concern
Box 33000
Seattle WA 98133

World Relief
1800 K St. NW
Suite 801
Washington DC 20006

World Vision International
P.O. Box "O"
Pasadena CA 91109

Y.M.C.A.
International Division
261 Broadway
New York NY 10007

Appendix 6

**INDOCHINESE REFUGEES SETTLED IN THE UNITED STATES
SINCE THE FALL OF SAIGON IN APRIL 1975
STATISTICS AS OF FEBRUARY 29, 1980**

State	Total Number of Refugees Resettled	State Population (1977 estimate)	Refugees Per Number of Inhabitants
Alabama	1,673	3,690,000	1:2,206
Alaska	251	407,000	1:1,622
Arizona	2,315	2,296,000	1:992
Arkansas	2,336	2,144,000	1:983
California	103,755	21,896,000	1:211
Colorado	6,579	2,619,000	1:398
Connecticut	2,869	3,108,000	1:1,083
Delaware	182	582,000	1:3,198
District of Columbia	3,560	712,000	1:200
Florida	6,672	8,452,000	1:1,267
Georgia	2,931	5,048,000	1:1,722
Hawaii	4,885	895,000	1:183
Idaho	539	857,000	1:1,590
Illinois	11,110	11,245,000	1:1,012
Indiana	2,898	5,330,000	1:1,839
Iowa	5,166	2,879,000	1:557
Kansas	4,072	2,326,000	1:571
Kentucky	1,519	3,458,000	1:2,276
Louisiana	9,401	3,921,000	1:417

(continued)

Appendix 6 (continued)

State	Total Number of Refugees Resettled	State Population (1977 estimate)	Refugees Per Number of Inhabitants
Maine	476	1,085,000	1:2,279
Maryland	3,260	4,139,000	1:1,270
Massachusetts	3,492	5,782,000	1:1,656
Michigan	5,500	9,129,000	1:1,660
Minnesota	9,085	3,975,000	1:438
Mississippi	1,033	2,389,000	1:2,313
Missouri	2,904	4,801,000	1:1,653
Montana	912	761,000	1:834
Nebraska	1,813	1,561,000	1:861
Nevada	1,735	633,000	1:365
New Hampshire	212	849,000	1:4,005
New Jersey	2,682	7,349,000	1:2,740
New Mexico	1,364	1,190,000	1:872
New York	8,795	17,924,000	1:2,038
North Carolina	2,775	5,525,000	1:1,991
North Dakota	525	653,000	1:1,244
Ohio	4,360	10,701,000	1:2,454
Oklahoma	4,886	2,811,000	1:575
Oregon	9,072	2,376,000	1:261
Pennsylvania	12,912	11,785,000	1:912
Rhode Island	1,886	935,000	1:496
South Carolina	1,126	2,876,000	1:2,554
South Dakota	580	689,000	1:1,188
Tennessee	2,988	4,299,000	1:1,439
Texas	30,065	12,830,000	1:427
Utah	3,527	1,268,000	1:360
Vermont	87	483,000	1:5,552
Virginia	8,789	5,135,000	1:584
Washington	12,596	3,658,000	1:290
West Virgina	272	1,859,000	1:6,835
Wisconsin	4,231	4,651,000	1:1,099
Wyoming	227	406,000	1:1,789

The last column is a calculation based on each state's total population divided by the total resettlement in that state. This figure indicates the number of refugees per capita in each state and provides a basis for comparing refugee resettlement rates from state to state. It should be noted, however, that these statistics use as a base the U.S. Immigration and Naturalization Service's January 1979 alien registration figures, plus the total number of new refugees who have arrived in each of these states since that time. The statistics, therefore, do not reflect any internal migration (i.e., movement from one state to another once a refugee has arrived in his/her first city of resettlement) that has occurred since January 1979. Hence, the error factor is considered to be significant.

(Data provided by Indochina Refugee Action Center, Washington, D.C.)

A Selected Bibliography

Carliner, David. *The Rights of Aliens.* New York: Avon Books, 1977.

Cherne, L. *A Personal Recollection: IRC Citizens Commission on Indochinese Refugees.* New York: International Rescue Committee, March 1978.

Davis, Kingsley. "The Migration of Human Populations," in *The Human Population.* New York: Scientific American, 1974.

Glazer, Nathan, and Moynihan, Daniel P. *Beyond the Melting Pot.* Cambridge: Harvard University Press, 1963.

Harper, Elizabeth J. *Immigration Laws of the United States.* 3d ed. New York: The Bobbs-Merrill Company, 1975.

Holborn, Louise W., et. al. *Refugees, a Problem of Our Time: The Work of the United Nations High Commissioner for Refugees, 1951–1972.* Metuchen, N.J.: Scarecrow Press, 1975.

———. *The International Refugee Organization: A Specialized Agency of the United Nations: Its History and Work.* London: Oxford University Press, undated.

Immigration and Naturalization Service. *Annual Reports of the Immigration and Naturalization Service.* Washington.

Intergovernmental Committee for European Migration. *ICEM: In Facts.* Geneva: ICEM, 1978.

International Refugee Organization. General Council. *Report of the Director General, 1 July 1948–30 June 1949.* Geneva: United Nations, 1949.

———. ———. *Annual Report of the Director General for the Period 1 July 1950 to 30 June 1951.* Geneva: United Nations, 1951.

Keegan, K. "Indochinese Refugees." *The New Republic,* 23 July 1977, pp. 11–12.

Liu, William T., et. al. *Transition to Nowhere: Vietnamese Refugees in America.* Nashville: Charter House Publishers, 1979.

Murphy, H.B.M. *Flight and Resettlement.* Lucerne: UNESCO, C.J. Bucher, 1955.

Piros, Mark, ed. *The Disillusioned: Twelve Million Refugees from Communism.* New York, 1959.

Pugash, James Z. "The Dilemma of the Sea Refugee: Rescue Without Refuge," *Harvard International Law Journal* 18: 577–604.

Schechtman, Joseph B. *European Population Transfers, 1939–1945.* New York: Russell & Russell, 1971.

———. *The Refugee in the World: Displacement and Integration.* New York: A.S. Barnes and Company, 1963.

Schwartz, Abba P. *The Open Society.* New York: Simon and Schuster, 1968.

Skinner, Kenneth A., and Hendricks, Glenn L. "Indochinese Refugees: An Emerging Ethnic Minority," paper presented at the 77th Annual Meeting of the American Anthropological Association, November 14–18, 1978, Los Angeles, Ca.

Speer, John K. "America's Post War Refugee Measures," *Interpreter Releases,* Vol. 48, No. 3, January 25, 1971. New York: American Council for Nationalities Services.

United Nations High Commissioner for Refugees. *United Nations Plan for Refugees.* Geneva: United Nations, 1955.

U.S. Library of Congress. Congressional Research Service. *Refugees in the U.S.: Laws, Programs, and Proposals* (by Catherine McHugh), Issue Brief No. IB77120. Washington: Library of Congress, November 2, 1978.

U.S. President's Advisory Committee on Refugees. *Final Report to the President.* Washington: January 1976.

Woodbridge, George. *The History of the United Nations Relief and Rehabilitation Administration.* Vols. 1, 2, and 3. New York: Columbia University Press, 1950.

Index